The Holy Grail
Source of the Ancient Science and Spirituality of the Circling Cosmos

Lee Perry

Saoirse Cainte Press
Cumming, Georgia
1993

The Holy Grail:
Source of the Ancient Science and Spirituality
of the Circling Cosmos

A paper presented to the
Calendar Conference
sponsored by the
Traditional Cosmology Society
and the
Northern Studies Centre
at Stromness, Orkney Islands, Scotland,
on June 20–22, 1993.

First edition published in 1993;
second edition in 1995 by
Saoirse Cainte Press
Cumming, Georgia, U.S.A.

Electronically typeset by LazerAge
Atlanta, Georgia, U.S.A.

ISBN: 1-883321-04-2
Library of Congress Catalog Card Number: 93-92645
Second Edition

Contents

Acknowledgments

This short book or long paper exists because my friend, Charles Newton Hooper, insisted that I write it. If it is free of typographical errors, you should thank Charlie Hooper. If not, blame me.

My mentor and friend, Charles Longstreet Weltner, a lifetime smoker, died of cancer last year, but his inspiration and humor lives on in **The Concilium of San Pietro**, an appendix to this work.

Tigger, my *pangar ban*, who is tabby not white, provided late-night companionship, as he did with my last book, *The Holy Grail, Cosmos of the Bible*. I swear that cat knows what I am at.

And last, but not least, thank you, God, for allowing me to find the *greille*, and to write about it.

Dedication

This work is for Carole, my wife; Kevin and Steven, my children who are with God; and Bruce, Brendan, and Conor, my living children.

ℭhe ℌolg ℭrail
Source of the Ancient Science
and Spirituality of the Circling Cosmos
Lee Perry

H oward Carter found the quintessential *material* treasure when he discovered the tomb of Pharaoh Tutankhamen. I found the quintessential *scientific* and *spiritual* treasure when I stumbled, fumbled, and fell into a rediscovery of the Holy rail. Howard Carter exposed his find for everyone to see, and they w. I published my find for everyone to read, but some academi- ans, as well as most persons with lesser amounts of education, rned their heads and walked away.

I made a big mistake. Having stumbled, fumbled, and fallen to a rediscovery of the Holy Grail quite by accident, I assumed at most people are sufficiently mature to learn what first- ntury Christians knew about the origins of their religion in the lendric science of the skies. Events occurring during the last vo years have proven that my assumption about human intellec- ial maturity was wrong.

The legendary Welsh knights of the colophon to *Perlesvaus*,[1] ne of the principal Grail romances, understood human nature r better than I. The *Perlesvaus* colophon tells us that two nights overcame their fear of the Christian clergy's warnings to tay away from the ruins of the Grail castle. The knights lived mong those ruins, where they rediscovered the secrets of the rail. Instead of returning to human society to tell everyone bout their rediscovery, they became hermits in the woods, voiding all contact with other humans. They knew that some cademicians, as well as most lay persons, have been brain- vashed by the Pauline Christian church so they will reject the cience, as well as the religion, of the Nazoreans (or Nazareans) vho followed the man we call "Jesus." Rather than being rejected y brainwashed humans, as I have been, the Welsh knights ejected the whole of Christianized humanity. In retrospect, I elieve their actions were more appropriate than mine.

I should have had better sense than to spend over ten years of my life and a substantial amount of my money researching, writing, and trying to publicize my book, *The Holy Grail, Cosmos of the Bible.* Having grown up in a family of engineers who had discovered or had invented various items and processes of relative importance in modern society, I should have realized that even the slightest innovation is regarded by some element of the power structure as a threat to its wealth, prestige, and power. Hence, the innovator must expect that all news about his innovation will be censored and suppressed by persons in power, unless, of course, the power structure believes that it can use the innovation to increase its own wealth, prestige, and power.

Candle makers surely did not applaud Thomas Edison's invention of America's first commercially-saleable light bulb. Likewise, the Christian hierarchy cannot be expected to welcome the rediscovery of mathematically near-certain evidence indicating that portions of biblical narrative they insist are inerrant history of fact are, instead, inerrant history of visionary experiences. Most especially is that rediscovery not welcome because the church's hierarchy did everything within its power, including crusades and inquisitions, to remove that evidence from human consciousness, and to preclude its rediscovery forever.[2]

One problem that the Christian hierarchy has in keeping their sheep in their pens, easily can be recognized. Except, perhaps, for those Christian fundamentalists whose minds are totally impacted with church dogma, most modern Christians quickly realize that a rock hurled directly at a visionary wee beastie hits something else, for the simple reason that a vision is present in appearance only, rather than in reality. According to a radio news report, a Christian fundamentalist recently confronted the distinction between fact and vision when a pot he hurled at a naked couple in a pornographic film being shown on television hit not the bare body of a living human being but the offending television tube. The Bible tells us that the risen Christ repeatedly "appeared" to his true believers.[3] Did the original Christians understand those "appearances" to have been visionary?

A fact is one thing. A vision is something else. The distinction is hard to escape, even to those blinded, deafened, and dumfounded by unreasoning religious faith. Grail-story authors uniformly were of the opinion that Christian knights would cease their combats with each other, and with Moslem knights, were they to realize that they were killing each other over visions that seers had seen among optical illusions appearing within a pattern of lines.[4] How this relates to the current genocide in Bosnia-Hercegovina soon will be discussed in this paper.

The Bible often states explicitly that what was seen by some seer was a vision.[5] I suggest that the Bible does not misinform us when it fails to label as visionary that which people of biblical times customarily regarded as visionary. In our own times, we assume everyone knows that stories about Mickey Mouse and Donald Duck are allegorical or metaphorical; are teaching parables, as well as amusements or entertainments. If some future generation chooses, for reasons that would make no sense to any of us, to believe that those cartoon characters actually lived and breathed, then the resulting problems cannot be laid upon the doorstep of Walt Disney.

My mistake was in assuming that the mind-control system of the Christian Church no longer is effective to herd people into separate denominational pens, there to control and to limit the quality and quantity of their spiritual feeding. I incorrectly assumed that people who are interested in God[6] tend nowadays to roam freely upon the mountaintops of spirituality with neither a shepherd nor a herd dog to control their spiritual direction or feeding. I incorrectly assumed that mind-control systems nowadays are the sole prerogatives of governments, business ventures, and pseudo-sciences.

According to my personal religious beliefs, my personal God would not authorize or permit the perpetual punishment of human beings who failed to obey the church's dogmas during their earthly existences. However, having graduated from an engineering school and a law school rather than from a religious seminary, I had not reckoned with the fact that many, if not most, modern Christians believe in a God who will punish them forever if they stray as much as an inch from the straight and narrow line drawn by the Christian clergy at the behest of the Christian hierarchy.[7]

Perhaps the stridency of the foregoing discussion can be softened somewhat if you will permit me to paraphrase your most famous bard, who hoped that we might see ourselves as others see us. To this end, I offer what I hope are two somewhat amusing true stories.

A Victorian-era, Christian lady of considerable wealth and position, whose name shall not be mentioned in this paper, once remarked: "I do hope Mr. Charles Darwin's theory of the evolution of the species is wrong, but if it is right, then I hope it never becomes widely known." Karl Marx similarly defined "truth" as that which advanced another cause he supported, a system of economics which, like Nazi totalitarianism, had many of the mind-control devices and external trappings of a religion.

A world-famous expert on the subject of electricity once declaimed: "What can that railroad clerk possibly know about electricity?" The railroad clerk was Thomas Alva Edison, the inventor of America's first commercially-saleable electric light bulb. The story perhaps indicates that academicians, like "hill-billy" farmers in the mountains of the State of Georgia, U.S.A., become very angry when they find outsiders trespassing in their fields. Most particularly are academicians infuriated if the trespasser is an "amateur" instead of "professional." But have you ever noticed how many important breakthroughs were made by amateurs, simply and solely because their minds were not totally impacted, or even clouded, by the tribal dogmas of some society of professionals? More about that later.

I have sent a summary of my conclusions and supporting evidence to many newspapers, news magazines, trade or professional journals, and radio and television stations in the United States, Great Britain, Ireland, and France. All have declined to mention a word about my work. Some have given me their reasons. Some representatives of the news media and academic societies refuse to publish or to broadcast anything contrary to their personal religious beliefs. Others are afraid of what might be called a "Salmon Rushdie" effect among Christian fundamentalists. They are afraid of rocks through their windows, or declining memberships, subscriptions, viewers, listeners, or commercial or charitable sponsors. Others express more lofty concerns, which boil down to a fear that all of western society will "come unglued" if people are presented with mathematically near-certain evidence indicating that portions of biblical narratives believed to be inerrant history of fact are, instead, inerrant history of visionary experiences. St. Paul wrote that Christianity is nothing if it is not entirely, factually true.[8] Christian fundamentalists believe it. And that ends all discussion, insofar as they are concerned.

The irony is that learned theologians and exegetes, and seminary-educated clergy, are almost universally of the opinion that my book contains "information which should be known by the people in the pews."[9]

Messrs. Lincoln, Leigh, and Baigent, of *The Holy Blood, and the Holy Grail* fame, have written extensively about the dichotomy between what the clergy say from the pulpit and what the clergy know.[10] They also have written extensively about the practical impossibility of the clergy's sharing the clergy's knowledge with the true believers in the pews.[11] If a clergyman says what he knows, as distinguished from what he knows his parishioners want and expect to hear, and his parishioners decline to believe him, then he may find himself out of a job, and his family on the dole. If, on the other hand, his parishioners believe what he tells them about the origins of Christianity among the calendric science of the skies, then his parishioners probably will abandon Christianity.

Congregations of Christians abandoning Christianity is precisely what is occurring with increasing frequency in the so-called "Torah Belt" within the so-called "Bible Belt" where I live in the Southeastern United States.[12] This astonishing mass exodus from Christianity is occurring among congregations of former Southern Baptists who have been exposed by their preachers to my writings, to those of Messrs. Lincoln, Leigh, and Baigent, as well as to those of others, such as Professors Ian Wilson and Hyam Mccoby.[13]

I anticipate that most of you are highly skeptical of my evidence and conclusions, and doubt that I have the academic qualifications to be presenting this paper to you this day. Excellent! Wonderful! If that is what is going on in your minds, you are possessed of sufficient scientific skepticism to stay with this presentation to the end. If your minds were totally impacted with religious dogma, you probably would have stormed out of the room long before now.

My qualifications, if any, to be before you today can be summarized during a brief exposition of how I stumbled, fumbled, and fell into a rediscovery of the Holy Grail. Following that, we shall consider the nature of the Grail, and the uses to which it was, and can be, put, which include, of course, its calendric functions.

There must be at least one Gaelic-speaker in the room today. Accordingly, although my childhood-learned Gaelic is rusty, and even badly decayed, I should have no difficulty in convincing you that *greille* is the Gaelic word for "grid" or "grill," and *grátáil* is the Gaelic word for "grille."[14] At least that is so among speakers of Irish Gaelic. Moreover, please permit me to remind you that every Grail scholar worth his or her salt will acknowledge the Celtic underpinnings of Grail tales. Moreover, although every person who has studied more than one language is familiar with the phenomenon that words spelled or pronounced similarly can have different meanings in different languages, I am of the opinion that you should not accuse me of being wholly irrational (or drunk on your fine whisky) because I am suggesting that we should allow Celtic words in Celtic stories to have Celtic meanings.

After the Albigensian Crusade, the Crusade against the Knights Templar, and the Inquisitions, the word "Grail" (spelled variously) came to mean "cup" or "chalice" in several continental romance languages.[15] The transition from "grid," "grill," or "grille" to "cup" or "chalice" may not have been the result of accidental mistranslation or misunderstanding of earlier oral or written Celtic tales. Rather, we may be considering the impact of the arrival from the east of the story of Joseph of Arimathaea's catching the blood of the crucified Jesus in the cup of the last supper.[16] Or, we may be viewing a deliberate attempt by the church triumphant to obfuscate or to obliterate what the Abbot Hélinand knew about the true nature of the Grail. In the year

1204, C.E., before the holocausts of crusade and inquisition, the good abbot described the Grail by use of the Latin words for a round leather shield, backed by a wickerwork lattice, which was a part of the accoutrements of a Roman foot soldier during a certain period of history.[17]

I believe no one present will deny that the English words "grid," "grill," "grille," and "lattice" can be used interchangeably to describe a pattern of lines that can be drawn or printed on a page. And I assume everyone here today will acknowledge that the Gaelic words for "chalice" (*cailís*) and for "cup" (*ballán, cuach,* or *cupán*) are sufficiently distinct from the Gaelic words for "grid" or "grill" (*greille*) and for "grille" (*grátáil*) so as to preclude an accidental confusion between cups or chalices, on the one hand, and grids, grills, or grilles, on the other.[18]

Although English-speakers probably will continue looking for the holy cup or chalice despite anything I say here today, I suggest that we Celts should commence a diligent search for the holy backyard barbecue grill, a concept perhaps as amusing as the holy hand grenade of Monty Python fame.

Thanks to great-grandfather James Morris, who tried to teach me the Irish and Welsh languages, I have known the probable meaning of the word "Grail" since early childhood.

We discussed earlier in this paper the problem with the tribal lore of societies of scholars. Fail to recite the tribal myth of your professional society *verbatim*, and you are apt to be shunned by, if not expelled from, the tribe. *If* conformity with the tribal myths of scholarly societies breeds mediocrity, then cross-fertilization of ideas between persons belonging to different scholarly disciplines is apt to result in irreconcilable conflict of ideas, on the one hand, or blending of ideas, on the other, depending upon the personalities and predilections of the persons involved in the academic alchemy. Although, because of our backgrounds, my mentor and I often found ourselves in conflict, our strengths and weaknesses were complementary, and we achieved together something that neither of us could have accomplished separately.

My mentor, Chief Justice Charles Longstreet Weltner of the Supreme Court of Georgia, died of cancer last year. Charles was well known in the United States as a champion of civil rights, as a consequence of which he received the Profile In Courage Award from the Kennedy Library Foundation. A trustee of Scholars Press, which publishes the writings of members of the Society of Biblical Literature and the American Academy of Religion, Charles was well known as a student of over a dozen ancient and modern languages, but few people realized that he also was a student of ancient mathematics, particularly geometry. In a scholarly paper, Charles speculated that a pattern of lines which fairly can be described as a "grid," "grill," "grille," or "lattice," that he had found on a panel of a Babylonian "algebraic-geometry" tablet dated to 1800-1600 B.C.E., *might* be related to the Prophet Ezekiel's visions because the pattern of lines on the tablet includes circles or wheels whose diameters or rims are inscribed with four eyes.[19] The tablet panel is depicted in **Illustration 1**. A circle or wheel with four eyes is depicted in **Figure 1**, by boldfacing certain of the lines of that tablet. From that seed, my studies grew.

Charles taught me to use "B.C.E." (before common era) in lieu of "B.C.," and "C.E." (common era) in lieu of "A.D.," in reference to time periods before and after the supposed birth date of Jesus. Now that I, too, am a member of the Society of Biblical Literature and the American Academy of Religion, I must engage in such "tribal-speak" to avoid raising the eyebrows of my academic brothers and sisters. You understand. If you rap, you are a brother!

Illustration 1—A geometry problem from a Babylonian cuneiform tablet of 1800 - 1600, B.C.E. Courtesy of the Trustees of the British Museum, London.

When Charles employed me as his law assistant, he knew that I am a graduate of Georgia Institute of Technology, grew up in a family of engineers, and earned some of my law-school tuition and expenses working as an engineering draftsman.

I asked Charles' permission to test his speculation by determining whether or not other verbal images appearing in the biblical narratives of Ezekiel's visions also might be found within that pattern of lines. One Friday night, I drew the pattern from the tablet on a piece of poster-paper, and proceeded to find within the pattern a line-form optical illusion corresponding to every verbal image from the biblical narratives of the prophet's two visions.[20] I drove to Charles' home the next morning, and showed him my findings. Neither he nor I had any idea what I had found. We knew nothing beyond the possibility that I had found something.

Charles suggested that I should read other biblical verses referring to the "cherubim" of Ezekiel's visions. Having spent the remainder of the weekend reading biblical stories containing the word "cherubim," I reported for work on Monday morning insisting that the verbal images of the stories of the Tabernacle, Ark of the Covenant, and Temple of Solomon probably were written in reference to line-form images appearing as optical illusions within the pattern of lines on the tablet.[21]

For months, I did not have any idea what I might have stumbled upon, even after finding the same phenomenon occurring among holy stories of many cultures, ancient and modern.[22] Then an image from an ancient Irish story[23] popped into my mind, leading me to reread that story of my youth, and to go where I knew it led me, i.e., to the original, unabridged versions of the stories of King Arthur and the quest for the Holy Grail.

I have asthma. My throat began to close as I read passages describing the Grail as an *achmardi*, i.e., a piece of precious green silk upon which a pattern of lines was sewn in gold threads,[24] and as I read narratives in which the hero and his lady sat down on a "rich silken cloth decorated with wheels,"[25] or "covered with wheeled patterns,"[26] or "on a carpet, finely decorated with flowers and animals."[27] This paper is too brief to summarize all of what I found in the unabridged manuscripts. Let me conclude this portion of the analysis by telling you that I had a massive asthma attack when I realized that the ancient Irish story containing the optical illusion I had recalled is a parody or satire on the Christ Story![28] I grabbed my inhaler, took several gulps more than prescribed, and,

Figure 1

as my ability to breathe slowly returned, I stumbled to the porch gasping to my wife that I had rediscovered the Holy Grail!

My always-skeptical wife looked at the line pattern, and told me that it is known among American colonial-style quilters as "cathedral window," if all of its straight lines and curved lines are sewn into the quilt, and is known as "double wedding ring," if only its circles are sewn.[29] My asthma attack returned at full intensity. The Holy Grail has been right before our eyes through the centuries! Years later, I found the writings of a student of Old French, who had predicted that when the Grail is rediscovered, humankind will be embarrassed to learn that it has been right under our noses, and within our gaze, all along.[30] That scholar also believes the Grail is a grid, grill, or grille, not a cup or a chalice. The Gaelic word *greille* apparently is a clone of the Old French word *greille*.[31]

Since then, my friends and I have found the *greille* in many churches in the United States, British Isles, and Europe, and on the remains of many ancient structures throughout Europe, the Middle East, and Asia. We even found it in a Pizza restaurant.

Please recall that I was graduated from an engineering school and a law school. I was not a student of the classics. A friend told me to look up the term "Mystery Religion" in an encyclopedia, and to read all books on the subject that I could find.[32] I learned that Christianity destroyed by fire and sword several mystery religions whose savior gods allegedly were born of a union between a sky god and an earth mother; who reputedly died and were born again; and whose faith promised that true believers would have life everlasting. I was born and raised in the Bible Belt, and had much to learn.

After publication of my book, I found that bookstores and libraries are full of books explaining how and why Christianity-- a new, im-proved, vegetation cult—became a system of mind- control with which to raise an army and to extend the Roman Empire. I shall not try to summarize those books in this short paper. Several are listed in my bibliography.[33]

How the Grail might be related to the very origins of the Christ Story comes into sharp focus when one realizes that the *Docetae*, i.e., Gnostic or Docetic Christians, typified by the Cathars, believed that the body of Christ was not of flesh and blood; rather that Christ's body was a "mere optical illusion."[34] Where and how the Gnostics said that Christ "appeared" is a topic we soon shall consider. Although modern Christian fundamentalists dislike Gnosticism, their favorite book of the Bible invariably is the Book of John, the Gnostic gospel.

The church's scribes rewrote books not burned during the thirteenth-century Albigensian Crusade and the Inquisitions that followed, when the people of the Holy Grail, the Cathars of southern France, whose claim to be the original Christians had historical merit, were slaughtered in battle, burned at the stake, or driven into the high mountains of Bosnia-Hercegovina, where they became nominal Moslems to gain protection from the Turks against Roman Catholic Croats and Eastern Orthodox Serbs bent on their total annihilation.[35] Look for a cause for the current insanity in Bosnia-Hercegovina and you will find Christians practicing genocide in the name of the God of us all. Blasphemy?

Scholars speculate that Wolfram von Eschenbach's Grail romance *Parzival* encodes a secret about the very origins of the Christ Story; a secret known as the treasure of the Cathars, and later known as the treasure of the Knights Templar, which may be the Holy Grail itself; a secret known to the clergy, which the clergy should keep to themselves, and should not share with the laity.[36] For instance, in the Grail romance *Perlesvaus*, presumably written in Wales by an anonymous Knight Templar, a priest in the Castle of Inquiry warned Sir Gawain, ". . . behoveth not discover the secrets of the Savior, and them also to whom they are committed behoveth keep them covertly."[37]

Messr. Ramon Lull, who spied on the Knights Templar in behalf of the King of France, said that those secrets were sufficient to "upset St. Peter's bark."[38] Lull's opinion has led to scholarly speculation that the Templars' knowledge of a devastating secret about the very origins of Christianity may have been one of many reasons for the annihilation of the Templars by the King of France, through crusade and inquisition, as well as one of many previous sources of the legendary wealth of the Knights Templar.[39]

This much we are told by the historians: During the night before the final assault by the armies of Rome on the Cathar fortress of Montségur, three or four highly-skilled mountain climbers brought the treasure of the Cathars down vertical cliffs hundreds of feet high and spirited it away through enemy lines.[40] Similarly, when the Templars received advance notice that the King of France was going to seize their Paris treasury, the treasure of the Templars quickly was spirited away to some unknown destination. Every Scot should know that destination *may* have been Scotland.[41]

Believe, if you must, that the English army ran away when a rag-tag party of camp followers joined King Robert the Bruce at Bannockburn.[42] Ignore, if your Christianity requires it, Rosslyn Chapel, and the dozens of Templar tombstones still extant in Scotland.[43] Or, instead, consider the suggestion that a treasure of precious metals and jewels could not have been so quickly and easily carried away and hidden, but a single piece of precious green silk upon which a pattern of lines had been sewn in gold threads easily would have been transportable and concealable. The history of the Cathars' defeat at Montségur includes a report that a piece of green cloth was brought down from the mountain by the night-time mountain climbers, and was spirited away to some unknown destination.[44] Why would a cloth be so valuable? We shall see the answer for ourselves.

Again, please accept my assurance that the many writings of Messrs. Lincoln, Leigh, and Baigent should help any Scot, freemason or not, to frame in what Grail lore is all about.[45] Those of you who have read everything those gentlemen have written have a distinct advantage over all others in attendance while we now take a few glances at some of what the Bible-era seers saw.

Would it be fascinating if latter-day seers still were seeing what Bible-era seers earlier had seen? I recently presented a paper to the International Society of Hildegard von Bingen Studies, suggesting that Hildegard, a Benedictine nun who lived from 1098 C.E. to 1179 C.E., could excoriate the Pope, and could demand that the Church return to several beliefs and practices of the "heretical" Cathars, without her being condemned and executed by the church's hierarchy, because she knew, in her own words, "the secrets of the heavenly mysteries"[46] that have been "hidden from the people,"[47] and because she demonstrated to the hierarchy her knowledge of the origins of the Christ Story in the calendric science of the sky by composing visions derived from optical illusions appearing to her within the lines of the *greille*.[48] In a few words, Hildegard blackmailed the church for its own good!

Grail stories state explicitly that the Grail was brought down to Earth from among the constellations of the sky.[49]

Hildegard stated specifically how her visions did, and did not, come to her: "I spoke and wrote these things [her visions] not according to the invention of my or any other person's heart, but as I saw, heard and perceived them in the heavens through the hidden mysteries of God."[50] What did Hildegard see in the heavens? Many images familiar to students of ancient cosmology and cosmogony, and to persons who have studied the Grail literature. Father Matthew Fox has suggested that there are connections between Hildegard's sky visions and Celtic-Hindu-Buddhist cosmology, the ancient mother-earth-goddess religions, the alchemical tradition, and world-axis symbolism which "goes back to pre-Neolithic times."[51] My book, *The Holy Grail, Cosmos of the Bible*, strongly supports Father Fox's suggestions about the breadth and depth of Hildegard's knowledge.

Thanks to the efforts of my friend Professor Bruce Hozeski of Ball State University, a formerly-obscure Medieval nun, Hildegard of Bingen, now is being appreciated as the quintessential feminist of human history. Any woman who did today what Hildegard accomplished during the twelfth century would be regarded as extraordinary. But Hildegard lived when the church-sponsored pall of ignorance was descending upon Europe, making Hildegard's achievements in the fields of physical and human sciences, medicine, music, and literature so remarkable that she may never be eclipsed by anyone.

We shall see a few examples of Hildegard's visions before we move along. Hildegard saw the sky as a jeweled tent "full of eyes," and saw Abraham, Isaac, Jacob, and John the Baptist as stars.[52] As you ladies and gentlemen know, stories about the comings and goings of ancient Semitic patriarchs or gods are apt to be stories about the apparent motions of stars in the sky because pre-biblical Hebrew religion regarded the stars as patriarchs who had become gods.[53]

A Christian commentator quoted in my book suggested that "there is not an incident in the whole Christ story that is not written in the stars."[54] A rabbi quoted in my book suggested that the richness and nuance of biblical narrative "is lost to biblical scholars who do not recognize the mythic origin of the message because they are ignorant of the astrological components of the Bible."[55]

In one of her visions, Hildegard saw in a "celestial illustration" a "kind of image which was filled with eyes."[56] How many "eyes" can you count in **Figure 1**? In another, she saw a wheel become visible in the center of the breast of a human figure she saw in the midst of the southern air.[57] As in **Figure 2**?

In still another of her visions, the last we shall discuss, Hildegard saw an image in the shape of a human, on an ivory plaque, on the breast of a young woman named "Lady," who brought forth the image from her womb before the daystar.[58] In his *History of the Church*, Eusebius of Caesaraea referred to Psalm 110 in an effort to prove to his readers that Jesus Christ was born a priest in the order of Melchizedek. Eusebius quoted from Psalm 110 as it read in his Bible, and still reads in the Vulgate Bible, as follows: "From the womb before the daystar I begat Thee."[59] You ladies and gentlemen know that the womb before the daystar, that is, before the Planet Venus while Venus is appearing as the "Morning Star," is a light phenomenon announcing the rising of the sun.[60] How could Eusebius have contended that Jesus Christ was born from the womb before the daystar and *also* was born of Our Lady? Because Our Lady had become the successor to all of the ancient sky goddesses by whose names the daystar previously had been known? And why do many modern Bibles make this less clear than did Eusebius' Bible and the Vulgate Bible? If the stories about the predecessor Queens of Heaven merely were sky stories, which were employed as features of a calendric system, then what might be implied about the new version of the narrative, in which only the names of the principal characters have been changed?

Perhaps, the effect upon us of our visions on the *greille* may be similar or identical to the effect that Hildegard's sky visions had upon

her. Hildegard wrote that after her visions, she "was able to understand books suddenly, the psaltery clearly, the evangelists and the volumes of the Old and New Testament..."[61] Hildegard apparently is saying essentially the same thing as the Christian and Hebrew commentators I quoted above. St. Hildegard cannot be regarded as a "heretic."[62]

Figure 2

If, once upon a time, the Christ Story was one of a long series of sky stories, used for calendric purposes, just how did that calendric system work? And what was its purpose?

Everyone present today knows that stellar periodicities, that is, the apparent movements of the stars across the posited biblical "firmament," "vault," or "dome" of the heavens, can be recorded in story form. A book by Messrs. Lorayne and Lucas, listed in the bibliography of this paper, teaches modern students a rather straightforward memory system which can be used instead of written mathematical notations to recall complex numerical data by encoding it in a story, then by decoding the story to yield the numerical data when it is needed. What Lorayne and Lucas teach modern students is one of the systems for remembering numerical data that was employed by the ancients before writing and mathematical notational systems were invented.[63]

I cannot pass this threshold without recalling the story of the Gaelic warrior and the Roman soldier who confronted each other bearing swords and shields, and sought to taunt each other with insults about who was, and who was not, a learned person. The Roman soldier shouted at the Gaelic warrior that the Gaelic warrior was ignorant because the Gaelic warrior neither could read nor write. The Gaelic warrior then shouted back that the Roman soldier was ignorant because the Roman soldier could not remember anything unless he wrote it down. Proving many things, I suppose, all of which are beyond the bounds of this paper.

So, we have made an important point. A sky story, that is, a story used to encode stellar periodicities, can be a calendar, a fact which I presume you already knew. And, as you already know, a calender in story form would be invaluable to early farmers and herdsmen, whose cycle of planting, tending, and harvesting of vegetable foodstuffs, and whose husbandry of animals, were governed by the cycle of the seasons. More than one book has been written about how various groups of farmers and herdsmen devised their own "vegetation cults," i.e., religions of sorts which defined the cycle of the seasons.[64]

I already have stated that there is a body of evidence indicating that Christianity originally was a new, improved vegetation cult.[65] Let me tantalize (or scandalize) you with just a few tidbits to that effect. Christ reputedly arose from the dead on the third day. So does the moon. Christ, as we have discussed, reputedly was born from the womb before the daystar. The cycle of the daystar over an eight-year period reconciles mathematically various calendric elements (heavenly bodies) that *apparently* move about the heavens, bringing, as it were, the calendar of the heavens back to zero every eight years, a fact known to the ancient Mayans as well as to the ancient Babylonians.[66] There even is some evidence that the Sumerians may have understood at least some aspects of the Venus cycle.[67]

Those of you who are devotees of ancient calendric systems probably are bored by what I am suggesting, and realize that I could carry on in this vein for hundreds of more pages. Christian fundamentalists surely do not want to consider the implications, and wish I would hush.

The Bible tells us that Christ was seized (harvested?), then was whipped and moved about (threshed and winnowed?), after which He was dried out on a cross. When He had died (dried?), He then was placed into a tomb (a granary?) from which He arose (as bread?) after passing by a circular stone (a mill stone?). And the church refers to His body as the bread of life. If Christ originally was a vegetation-cult god, He was not the first. The Egyptian Osiris, a grain god, was said to have "saved" humankind from anthropophagy, i.e., cannibalism.[68] Mythologists understand what Christian fundamentalists reject.

The ritual death of savior "kings," followed by the ritual consumption of their flesh and blood to "save" the rest of the tribe, was anything but a new concept when the Christ Story first was told.[69] And, as English-language translations of the Dead Sea Scrolls recently have revealed, the collection of beliefs and ceremonies that later became known as Christianity apparently is an archaic form of pre-Second-Temple Judaism, instead of an outgrowth of latter-day Rabbinical Judaism.[70] Taunts and jibes in the Grail tales about which is the old religion and which is the new religion reveal that Grail authors knew facts about Christian origins that only recently have been rediscovered when, after many years of lying about in the hands of church-sponsored translators, the Dead Sea Scrolls finally are available to the general public in English-language translations, thanks, in no small part, to an *exposé* by Messrs. Leigh and Baigent.[71] You can read about that subject in detail in my book, and others. Right now, please let me finally redeem my promise to show you what the seers saw.

What was (and is) the Holy Grail? Some people insist that the Grail was a cup, chalice, plate, bowl, or platter, although others insist that it was a religious book, a comb maker's file, or a wide variety of tangibles and intangibles.[72] Wolfram von Eschenbach, the Grail author who wrote explicitly that the Grail was an *achmardi*, also indicated that the Grail was a thin, flat stone, a jewel, upon which optical illusions of sacred persons, objects, symbols, and ceremonies appeared, then disappeared.[73] He was correct, as we soon shall see for ourselves.

In one sense, the Holy Grail is a pattern of lines that can be put to a variety of uses. Rocks or bricks stacked according to this pattern become the classical vaults and domes of houses of worship of many religions, past and present.

Illustration 2 depicts the four classical vaults in isometric perspective.[74] **Figures 3-6** reveal the presence of the four classical vaults within the lines of the *greille* in plan, profile,

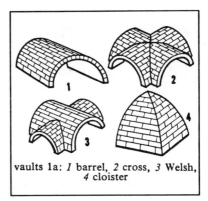

vaults 1a: *1* barrel, *2* cross, *3* Welsh, *4* cloister

Illustration 2—The four classical vaults. By permission. From Webster's Third New International Dictionary © 1986, at page 2536, *by Merriam-Webster, Inc., publisher of the Merriam-Webster® dictionaries.*

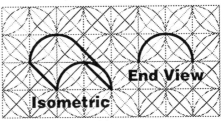

Figure 3

Figure 4

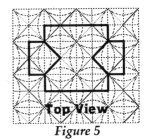

Figure 5

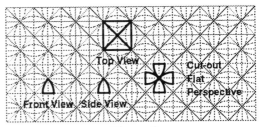

Figure 6

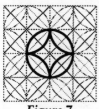

Figure 7

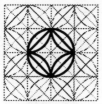

Figure 8

and isometric views. **Illustrations 3 and 4** depict in isometric perspective pendentives as the Byzantine Christian and Moslem geometrical solution to the architectural problem of setting a dome on a cubical supporting frame.[75] **Figures 7-8** depict on the *greille* in plan or top view the use of pendentives to support a dome on a square. Am I saying that the Grail was the source of these construction techniques? Yes and no. Stay with me only a few more minutes.

Anyone who really is familiar with the history of church architecture will tell you that the operative masons who erected the great cathedrals of Europe regarded the quartz crystal as the "microcosmos," regarded the posited

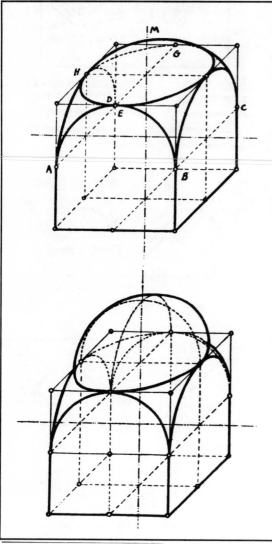

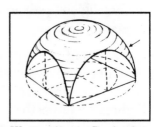

Illustration 3—The cuboctahedron as the Byzantine Christian and Moslem solution to the architectural problem of setting a dome on a cubical supporting frame. Courtesy of Dover Publications, Inc., New York.

Illustration 4—Pendentives supporting a dome on a square. Courtesy of Doreen Yarwood and Bounty Books, London.

"firmament" or dome of the sky as the "macrocosmos," and regarded the cathedral as the mean in between.[76] Although operative freemasonry, long before the advent of speculative freemasonry, was a secret society, the cathedrals have been "decoded" by modern architects and engineers,[77] and a few sketchbooks of the operative master masons have been found by modern scholars,[78] revealing beyond cavil one aspect of the real world of the Holy Grail.

The master masons discovered[79] that God had constructed the quartz crystal according to mathematical precepts.[80] The master masons expressed those constructs geometrically, using stereographic projections, plans, and profiles still used in modern mathematical crystallography.[81] They used those constructs to erect cathedrals, God's house on earth, according to the principles used by God in creating the quartz crystal.[82] Next, they projected those lines onto the "firmament" or dome of the heavens, and they, and early astronomer-astrologers, used those mathematical constructs to calculate stellar periodicities, thereby constructing a great calendar in the sky.[83] Nonsense, you say. Really? Open your eyes and see for yourselves what the seers saw.

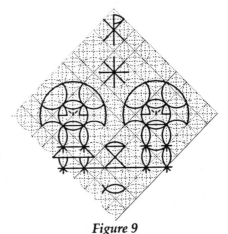

Figure 9

Illustration 5 is a black-and-white copy of the rainbow- colored uniaxial interference pattern which can be viewed by naked eye when the sun strikes a thin slice of quartz crystal.[84] Ah, Wolfram, you knew so much more than modern teachers who use abridged translations of your poetry in their English-literature classes possibly could have imagined. You were more than a poet. You were a mathematician, schooled in the best Moorish science of your day. **Figure 9** depicts the uniaxial

Illustration 5—A black-and-white copy of a color photograph of the uniaxial interference pattern which can be viewed by the naked eye in quartz and other crystals. Note the misalignment of the circle at the fracture. Courtesy of Dover Publications, Inc., New York.

interference pattern on the *greille*, situate around the heads of a manform and a womanform, between whom appears (that word, again) a mangerform, below which appears a Christian fishform, and above which appear a Sumerian starform and a Christian Chi-Rho-form. Too much to swallow in one mouthful? Sorry. My book, *The Holy Grail, Cosmos of the Bible*, serves it up in small tidbits, but we are wanting for time and space in this paper.

Illustration 6—Muireachdach's Cross, Monasterboice, County Louth, Ireland. Courtesy of the Office Of Public Works, Republic of Ireland.

Are you ready for dessert? No Scot or Irishman needs to be told what **Illustration 6** depicts.[85] If you can endure my pun, de Picts seem to have known more about de Grail den de Papa in-a Rome could-a stomach. No wonder that when Scots of King Robert the Bruce's ilk were directed by the Romanized Christian clergy to look toward Rome, they saw, instead, visions of Iona.

I shall discuss one more use of the Grail in the construction of cathedrals by operative master masons, then we shall move directly to a discussion of the Grail as a calendar in the sky.

Illustration 7 depicts (no pun intended) another panel from the Babylonian school-boy's tablet upon which **Illustration 1** also appears.[86] **Illustration 8** depicts part of a

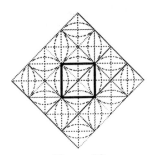

Figure 10   *Figure 11*   *Figure 12*

Illustration 7—Doubling the square, a geometry problem on the other side of the same ancient Babylonian tablet from which came Illustration 1. Courtesy of the Trustees of the British Museum, London.

Illustration 8—Doubling the square, from the sketchbook of a master mason. Courtesy of Michael Russell (Publishing) Ltd., Wilton, Salisbury, England.

page of an operative master mason's sketchbook.[87] **Figures 10, 11, and 12** depict on the *greille* the process, attributed by classical scholars to Plato, of "doubling the square."[88] The geometrical process is quite simple. Take a square, as in **Figure 10**. Construct within that square four identical triangles, as in **Figure 11**. Fold each of those four identical triangles outward, creating a larger square composed of eight identical triangles, as in **Figure 12**. The large square in **Figure 12** is twice the area of the small square in **Figure 10**.

If you think that modern algebra provides a better solution to this construct than ancient geometry, then take a 10-foot by 10-foot square of 100 square feet. Double it *in area*. Ouch! Sometimes, learning the hard way is the best way. Doubling the square not only allows a quick and easy doubling of the area of a space in a cathedral, but allows the proper construction of the church's steeple or spire. Please refer to **Illustration 9**, which depicts another cut from a master mason's sketchbook.[89] Starting on the left and progressing toward the right, we double the square. Then we rotate the slices, and center them upon each other. *Voila*! We have a plan or top view of sections of a church spire or steeple. Who said the Grail was poetic nonsense?

Classical scholars often accuse me of iconoclastically smashing their most beautiful constructs of reality. Plato figured out the geometry of doubling the square, the classicists insist.[90] Really? Then what is the procedure for doubling the square doing on a Babylonian algebraic-geometry tablet dating from 1800-1600 B.C.E.? Classicists also insist that Plato fathered the so-called "Platonic Solids," three-dimensional constructs also later used by master masons to erect the cathedrals of Europe.[91] Really? Examples of each of the "Platonic Solids," carved on stone balls long before the birth of Plato, have been found in the British Isles, as well as elsewhere across Europe.10[92] Then what about the so-called "Pythagorean Theorem" for the right-angle triangle? You recall that formula if you recall none other. In modern algebraic notation, $C^2 = A^2 + B^2$. In words, the square of the hypotenuse equals the sum of the squares of the other two sides. Another Babylonian tablet predating Pythagoras by hundreds of years illustrates the so-called "Pythagorean Theorem."[93] I have gone after mental constructs of the religionists with jackhammer and chain saw within the confines of this paper. It seems that the mental constructs of the mathematicians also require some demolition and reconstruction.

We have been discussing the question of what the Holy Grail really was and is. We have viewed for ourselves some evidence that in one sense it was and is a pattern of lines used to stack rocks or bricks in cathedral constructs replicating the quartz crystal. Operative master masons had the audacity to believe that they could erect a house for

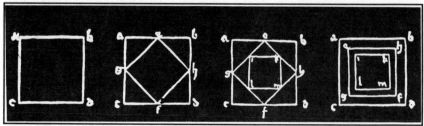

Illustration 9—Doubling the square to take an elevation from a plan. Courtesy of Michael Russell (Publishing), Ltd., Wilton, Salisbury, England.

God here on Earth using God's own principles of algebraic-geometry that would replicate what religionists and philosophers have referred to as "Heavenly Jerusalem."[94] That presumes a similar construct in the sky. To be specific, a similar construct on what the Greeks called the *katapetasma*. More later about what might be regarded, in modern terms, as the movie screen in the sky.

Simple but effective mathematics which led to the construction of large vaults and domes led to the speculation that Heaven had a vault or dome.[95] The Hebrews thought Heaven had a dome of ice upon which God sat enthroned, opening and closing the sluice gates of the waters of Heaven.[96] In that way did they explain rain.[97]

Are biblical sluice gates in an ice dome that are opened and closed by an enthroned God what we would call "science," or what we would call "religion"? Ancients like the biblical Hebrews did not differentiate between science and religion.[98] Thus, the practical impossibility of my discussing calendric science separately and apart from visionary religion. Everyone is bound to know that the Bible is a hotch potch of both science and religion. For instance, Hebrew religionists insisted that 3.0 is the correct value for π.[99] Hebrew mathematicians knew better, but had to bury their knowledge in the numerology of the tabernacle perceived in the sky. Twenty-two sevenths (3.14) is our modern value for π. Hebrew mathematicians used twenty-two sevenths as the value of π.[100] They just could not discuss it openly, because their religious pundits insisted that π must come out even.[101] Why do we continue singing about the sun's coming up in the morning? Don't we know better?

In so-called Pythagorean mathematics, in which the Hebrew sages were true believers, the numbers one and two are not numbers; rather, they are constructs of numbers. Three is the first Pythagorean number, a construct of one and two.[102] Three is one? The Trinity? I wish we had time to learn that biblical numerology is not always nonsense, as "educated persons" these days so contemptuously and ignorantly assume and assert.

When early Christians stated that the Bible is inerrant, I believe they meant that its allegories, metaphors, and parables encode the same mathematics from God that the master masons used to construct the cathedrals of Europe. I contend that operative master masons were encoding and decoding in stone the same data about God's creation, the same cosmology and cosmogony, that the Christian clergy were encoding in biblical allegories, metaphors, and parables. Is the love-hate relationship between Christianity and speculative freemasonry naught but a brotherly pillow fight that occasionally erupts into an exchange of fists, producing a later-regretted bloody nose? When that sibling relationship gets out of hand, does Cain still slay Able, or the master mason still slay his apprentice, for no better reason than children in Belfast's brickyards bloody each other's noses, i.e., to prove who is king of the brick pile? Are we better than, the same, or worse than the animals?

Radical Christian fundamentalists, whose stance about their religion is as pugilistic as the stance of Belfast's ragamuffins about their brick piles, nowadays take "biblical inerrancy" to mean that all biblical narratives are without a single flaw, despite the fact that *most* fundamentalists would not dare to erect their churches using 3.0 as the value of π. A neighbor of mine who is a psychiatrist refers to that state of mental dissociation as "cognitive dissonance." The most radical Christian fundamentalists in one Bible-Belt state in the United States tried to mandate through legislation the use of a π of 3.0 on all construction projects within the state, but, fortunately, the professors of mathematics hooted them down.[103]

Before you laugh or sneer at the biblical Hebrews because of the cognitive dissonance imposed by their religion, consider that as late as the eighteenth century, Europeans quite extensively, although Scots and Irish to a much lesser extent, caused the murder of innocent women they sincerely believed were witches.[104] The King James Bible says there are witches, and that witches should not be suffered to live.[105] Forgetting their common humanity, Christians believed and obeyed. Fortunately, we no longer burn women as witches, but you may rest assured that we do other things based upon our present-day theories of science and religion that will amuse and disgust future generations, who will wonder how we could have been so stupid. Here is the point: Let any of us who is without silly beliefs about science and religion throw the first snide remark at the ancient Hebrews because their religion mandated that certain scientific precepts be buried in building constructs rather than discussed openly. Scots, in particular, should not forget Rosslyn Chapel![106]

The pattern of lines of the Grail, when projected upward onto the posited "firmament" or "dome" of Heaven, and downward onto the round Earth, led to systems for finding points in time-space on the presumed curvature of Heaven and on the known curvature of earth; that is, to mathematical astronomy, and to land and ocean navigation.[107] I shall whisk right past most details of the navigational uses of the Grail, after assuring you that the Grail still is painted all over buildings and inscribed on beaches in the New Hebrides Islands, now known as the Republic of Vanuatu, near Australia,[108] and still is used by open-boat sailors for accurate star-sight navigation between Tahiti and the Hawaiian Islands. The British Museum contains details, and a program recently run on American public television covered extensively one such successful voyage. Read my book.[109]

Do you remember the ancient concept of the quartz crystal as microcosmos, the sky as macrocosmos, and the cathedral as the mean in between? All three aspects were critical when we discussed cathedral construction. Now, we need to discuss the crystallography of the posited "dome" of the sky and the known curvature of the earth.

Illustration 10 depicts a stereographic projection of a quartz crystal.[110] I must remind you that we are not considering the sort of hocus-pocus crystallomancy found in New Age religious literature. If "religion" is that which we *will not* subject to rational analysis, and "science" is that which we *will* subject to systematic skeptical inquiry, then "magic" might be defined as religion and science run amuck. We are discussing modern

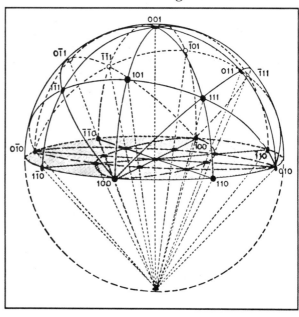

Illustration 10—Stereographic projection of a crystal. Courtesy of Dover Publications, Inc., New York.

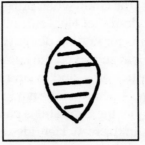

Illustration 11—Early Sumerian pictograph for "star," "heaven," or "god." Courtesy of the University of Chicago Press, Chicago.

Illustration 12—Early Sumerian pictograph for "Earth," i.e. the planet, not the soil. Courtesy of the University of Chicago Press, Chicago.

Illustration 13—Early Sumerian pictograph for "mountain." Courtesy of the University of Chicago Press, Chicago.

mathematical crystallography, as well as ancient mathematical crystallography.

Assume that the top half of the sphere in **Illustration 10** depicts the posited "firmament" or "dome" of Heaven. Curved lines on the "dome" become straight lines on the stereographic projection that separates the top half of the sphere from the bottom half of the sphere.[111]

No one ever has succeeded in proving how ancient mathematicians could solve problems which we would approach through spherical geometry and spherical trigonometry. We know they did solve them. We just do not know how. In his tome on the subject, Professor Hapgood assumed that the ancients either could work three-dimensional problems, or had a method for reducing three-dimensional problems to two-dimensional problems, which we know they had the mathematical tools to solve.[112] Stereographic projections are one way of reducing three- dimensional problems to two-dimensional problems. Stereographic projections, of the sort depicted in **Illustration 10**, are the tools that open-boat navigators still use when they chart star risings on the grid, grill, grille, or lattice of a platted reed mat using sea shells as locators. Again, who among us has insisted that the Grail is poetic nonsense?

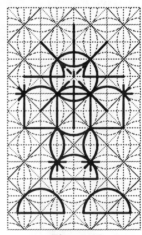

Figure 13

Lee Perry

Now that we know that points on a dome can be projected down as straight lines onto a plane stereographic projection, we need to look for a moment at what Professor Samuel Noah Kramer tells us are among the oldest written symbols in the world. **Illustration 11** is the early Sumerian pictograph for "star," "heaven," or "god."[113] You should know that **Illustrations 11-13** are not my drawings. Instead, they are photographic images of drawings in one of Dr. Kramer's books. **Illustration 12** is the early Sumerian pictograph for "Earth," i.e., the planet not the soil.[114] **Illustration 13** is the early Sumerian pictograph for "mountain."[115]

What do we see in **Figure 13**? English-language translations of the Moses Story indicate that when Moses came down from "the mountain," the skin of his face "shone."[116] Our manform optical illusion in **Figure 13** stands on the early Sumerian pictograph for "mountain," and his face is shining with the rays of the Sumerian pictograph for "star" or "god." What does he hold in his arms?

American Indians learned that the sun's reverse image safely can be viewed by allowing the sun's rays to pass through a narrow opening in or between rocks, and to fall upon a rock surface. Functional examples of such sun-viewing stations, which were used by tribal shamans to establish the arrival of the solstices and the equinoxes, are to be found throughout North America.[117] The King James version of Exodus 33:20-23 describes this technique. The shaman stands at a predetermined location. Exodus 33:21 says, "[T]hou shalt stand upon a rock." The sun's rays penetrate between the rocks or through a man-made hole. Exodus 33:22 says, "[W]hile my glory passeth by... I will put thee in a clift of the rock." The translation of Exodus 33:22 in the New English Bible employs the word "crevice" instead of "clift." The shaman views the reverse image of the sun projected onto a rock. Exodus 33:23 says, "[A]nd thou shall see my back parts: but my face shall not be seen." My book, *The Holy Grail, Cosmos of the Bible*, goes more deeply into this analysis. Limitations of time and space in this paper demand that we now turn to other calendric aspects of biblical sky science.

Who among us has not heard something about Ezekiel's wheel in the middle of a wheel? One problem immediately confronts us. The Hebrew does not say, "in the middle of." The Hebrew word is *betoch*, which the New English Bible correctly translates as "inside."[118] The difference between the specific "in the middle of" and the unspecific "inside" poses the interesting question of how King James' translators knew exactly where one wheel was in reference to the other wheel, although the Hebrew does not say. Could it be that they knew what Ezekiel was writing about, whereas many of us do not?

I assume that you ladies and gentlemen are not altogether unfamiliar with classical geometry. What do we see in **Illustration 14**?[119] Stay with me, because we are about to strike the mother lode, i.e., the truth which the church feared Galileo might reveal to Christian true believers were he not silenced by death or lifetime imprisonment.[120]

Illustration 14 is a mathematics professor's sketch of a "concave-sided tetragon," i.e., the geometric form that has been with us since we first viewed an image on the *greille* in **Figure 1**.[121] Persons who are mathematically inclined refer to that pattern of lines as a "hypocycloid," or, even more specifically, as an "asteroid."[122] However, for our purposes, it is more important what that geometric figure will do than the name by which it is known. We are nearing the top of the mountain. Do not cheat yourself by giving up and turning back. Press on to enjoy the view from the top.

A hypocycloid is a curve generated by a mark on the circumference of a circle which rolls on the inside of [i.e., *betoch*] the circumference of a fixed circle.[123] There is a cusp at every point where the mark touches the fixed circle. See **Figure 1**. A four-cusped hypocycloid is known as an asteroid.[124]

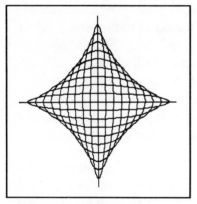

Illustration 14—The concave-sided tetragon as an envelope of ellipses. Courtesy of Dover Publications, Inc., New York.

An asteroid can serve as an "envelope of ellipses."[125] According to one of Kepler's theorems, the planets travel around the sun at variable velocities along flight-paths resembling ellipses.[126] Sir Fred Hoyle, one of your finest astronomers, believes the "Aubrey Circle" at Stonehenge represents the Ecliptic.[127] Many stone "circles" in Great Britain are not circles at all; rather, they contain elliptical elements.[128] Were the ancients of Britain attempting to state in stones what

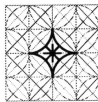
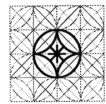
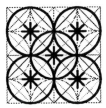

| *Figure 14* | *Figure 15* | *Figure 16* |

Kepler later stated in words and mathematics, i.e., the speculation that the planets travel in elliptical orbits around the sun? If so, they arguably were millennia ahead of the master masons who erected the cathedrals of Europe!

Is Ezekiel expressing the opinion that the rotation of the Earth around the Ecliptic or Zodiac (one wheel) as the Earth rotates around itself (the other wheel) can be described on the ground and in the sky by an envelope of ellipses?[129] Did Kepler construct for himself his speculation that the planets travel around the sun in elliptical orbits, or did he inherit it from his mother, whom the church had burned at the stake as a witch?[130]

Here we go for the summit. **Figure 14** depicts an early Sumerian pictograph for "star," which is located in the middle of an envelope of ellipses. Is this a line drawing of our sun in the middle of the rotational orbits of the planets? **Figure 15** depicts an early Sumerian pictograph for "star" in the middle of four early Sumerian pictographs for "Earth," i.e., the planet not the soil. Is this a line drawing of our planet orbiting our sun? **Figure 16** depicts one Sumerian pictograph for "star" centering each of four circles, which, in turn, are centered by the pictographs and geometrical forms of **Figure 14** and **Figure 15**. Does **Figure 16** depict one "Guardian Star" within each of the four colures, the planet Earth at each of its four seasonal positions opposite the solstices and equinoxes, and the sun within the elliptical orbits of the planets? Is **Figure 16** a pictographic stereographic projection of our solar system? I may have lost some of you on that **Figure 16** burst of speed to the top of the mountain. Let me come back down and give you a hand up.

In the astronomy of the ancients, the twelve divisions of the Zodiac were fixed along the Ecliptic by four "Guardian Stars," also referred to as the "Tetramorphs," "Royal Stars," "Archers," or "Watchers."[131] Those four stars define a cross in the sky.[132] They are Regulus, lying in the constellation Leo (the *lion*), Aldebaran, lying in the constellation

Taurus (the *bull*), Fomalhaut, now lying in the Southern Fishes but formerly considered to be lying in the constellation Aquarius (the water- bearing *man*), and Antares, lying in the *former* constellation of the *eagle*, which now is more or less the constellation Scorpio, the scorpion.[133] They are Lion, Ox, Man, and Eagle, the Tetramorphs of Ezekiel's visions and the symbols chosen by the Christian church for the four evangelists.[134] The Christian order is: Matthew—the winged man; Mark—the winged lion; Luke— the winged ox; and John—the eagle.[135]

Here is the crux of the matter: Within extended periods of time during the precession of the Equinoxes, certain of those four stars served, more or less, as locators of the solstices and equinoxes.[136] For instance, Aldebaran more or less marked the vernal equinox from approximately 4000 B.C.E. to approximately 1700 B.C.E., the latter date being within the precessional "window" of our Babylonian tablet.[137] The four Guardian Stars were used to locate the equinoctial and solstitial colures, four great circles in the sky.[138] Now, you are ready to sprint to the top of the mountain.

Look again at **Figure 16**. Four colures centered by four Guardian Stars, fixing the two solstices and the two equinoxes along the Ecliptic or Zodiac? Planet Earth at each of its four seasonal positions, directly opposite the four Guardian Stars which center the four colures and fix the solstices and equinoxes? All of that centered by an envelope of ellipses, defining the rotational paths of the planets, which is centered by the sun? Are we observing a pictographic stereographic projection of the sun-centered cosmos of Aristarchus of Samos?

Did precession do to this early unified theory of the cosmos what quantum physics and the mathematics of chaos have done to Sir Isaac Newton's clockwork universe? Or did the church drive this theory into the closet for centuries in order to preserve and to protect ecclesiastical power over the people?

I assume that you know about Aristarchus and his relationship with the Christian "heretics" Galileo and Kepler.

If not, we shall be brief about it.

Nearly everyone knows that the church silenced Galileo by placing him under house arrest for the remainder of his life rather than executing him for his expressed "heresy" about what centered what in the sky, and what rotated around what in the sky.[139] The modern church wants its true believers to believe that Galileo was the first to posit a sun-centered cosmos.[140] However, Galileo credited Copernicus, who credited Aristarchus, who credited "the ancients" with the first exposition of a theory and proof of the existence of a sun-centered cosmos.[141] And the church burned Kepler's mother as a witch.[142]

The question that must be burning in the craw of any Christian fundamentalist who has made it thus far into the dark recesses of this paper is: "Why did the church care what centered what in the sky, or what rotated around what in the sky?" The answer is quite simple. The church was, and wanted to remain, the sole authority on everything, including science as well as religion.[143] The church had sought to destroy the old science as well as the old religion because the two were inseparable.[144] Finding the old science quickly can lead a Christian true believer to the very origins of the Christian faith in the sky stories of the ancient calendric system.[145] The ancient libraries of the world had been burned by mobs of raging Christian fundamentalists at the behest of Christian clergymen, and the ancient scholars of science and mathematics had been stoned to death by raging mobs of Christian fundamentalists.[146] Then here came that "heretic" Galileo, using his homemade telescope to open the entire can of worms.[147] Can "heresy" never be suppressed?

Apparently, "heresy," i.e., heartfelt disagreement with the church's power structure, cannot ever be suppressed. The Cathars, whose destruction by crusade and inquisition was cut short by their flight to the mountains of Bosnia-Hercegovina, where Eastern Orthodox Serb Christians and Roman Catholic Croat Christians still are trying to annihilate them,[148] went to the fiery stake[149] rather than abandon the following fundamental precepts of religion and life-style: The Cathars were vegetarians.[150] They practiced birth control and abortion, in an effort to keep their numbers in balance with their environment.[151] They believed in equality between men and women, which led them to ordain women as well as men as their priests.[152] Worst of all—in the eyes of the church of Rome—the Cathars believed that everyone should have available a copy of the Bible, and should read it and interpret it for himself or herself, and that every believer had direct access to God in his or her prayers.[153] Unemployment for Roman priests would have been the result had Catharism (i.e., Puritanism) continued its rapid spread across the face of Europe.

What must the Holy Father think when he sees those "modern" issues coming across his desk on a daily basis? I admire and respect the Polish Pope as much as you Scots adore your Bonnie Prince, but, Irish imp that I am, I cannot help but chuckle when I think about the terrible tummy ache all of this "heresy" must give him! And, on top of it all, you Scots and your British associates now are suffering from royal scandals. Will the masses yet be free? What mists are arising from Culloden Moor? What flowers are growing in your forests?

Only recently has the women's movement in the United States found what happened to Hypatia, the daughter of Theon, a woman professor of mathematics whose commentaries are our only source of much of the work of Euclid and others. Hypatia was stoned to death by a raging mob of Christian fundamentalists because she would not give up her "heresy," i.e., mathematics.[154]

Can I assure you that **Figure 16** was intended as a stereographic projection of the sun-centered cosmos of Aristarchus of Samos? Of course not. The contents of this paper are speculations, backed up by such evidence as was not burned by the church when it destroyed the ancient libraries. However, my methods are not dissimilar to those of modern-day archaeologists, and to those of the famous archaeoastronomer, Dr. Gerald S. Hawkins, the man who decoded Stonehenge, a place replete with Grail-borne geometrical constructs.[155] Stonehenge was treated extensively in my book. Dr. Hawkins and I have corresponded. He apparently does not regard my methods as being unscientific or my conclusions as being ridiculous.

If a learned archaeologist may write "hide scraper" in his notebook to describe a flint chip he recovers from the burial of an archaic female, and Dr. Hawkins may label Stonehenge as a "Stone Age Computer," then why am I not entitled to write "line drawing of the solar system" in my book and in this paper? The answer is simple. Christianized society is not yet sufficiently mature emotionally and intellectually to deal effectively with my speculations and supporting evidence, and the rest of the world does not want to offend its wealthiest trading partner, the Christianized United States of America. Thus, the mistaken hermeneusis continues.

We have seen something of the Grail as architectural plan and profile for the construction of cathedrals. We have seen the Grail's use as a calendar in the sky. Next, we shall see the Grail as the visionary source of a religious mind-control system that produces genocide in Bosnia-Hercegovina and tolerates an oil-spill in the Shetlands. The Right Reverend John Shelby Spong, Episcopal Bishop of Newark, New Jersey, U.S.A., yearns for the day when Christians no longer will park their brains at the door before they enter the church building.[156] He is attempting to dismantle the mind-control system which the church's hierarchy established and maintained, being of the opinion that fundamentalism is destroying the church.

Warning! What follows is a teaching parable rather than a report of historical fact. (If only the authors of Bible stories always had so labeled their writings.)

Three ancients are huddled around a clay tablet upon which have been inscribed several repetitions of the pattern of lines on the *greille*. We cannot correctly say that one is an astronomer, one is a builder, and the third is a shaman because all three are shamans, builders, and astronomers. As you recall, what we separately pigeonhole as "science" and "religion" were undifferentiated aspects of priestly knowledge during times past. But we must give our storybook characters names for purposes of this parable, as in the Bible "Adam" became the name of a person instead of a handful of dirt, and "Eve" became his wife, instead of merely being water vapor. So I have named our priests-scientists "Astronomer," "Builder," and "Shaman," solely for ease of reference.

Astronomer, Builder, and Shaman are engaged in the task of erecting a house for a god. The time is the third millennium B.C.E., and the place is what we now call Iraq. The stars of the rotating cosmos are circling above their heads, offering sufficient light to illuminate their work.[157] For inspiration, each has had a little nip of a narcotic plant. Do not be shocked. Narcotic substances were used everywhere during those days as a source of what we would call "spiritual" or "religious" inspiration.[158] The substance of which our three persons have partaken is your societal equivalent of an evening cup of tea or a "small one" of *uisce beatha*.

Using the *greille*, Astronomer and Builder are laying down on the ground the foundation lines of the structure and are aligning it with the cosmos. Shaman is comparing the lines of the *greille* on the tablet with the lines of the *greille* on the stereographic projection in the sky. Shaman is about to have a vision. As I am not familiar with the terminology that Shaman would have used, I must rely upon the words later used by Greek-speakers to describe the mechanics of Shaman's vision.

In a vision, Shaman thinks that he sees a boundary (*horos*) between Heaven and Earth, over which is stretched a veil or curtain (*kátapetasma*), onto which are projected, by the Creator God in Heaven, the secret patterns (*paradeigmata*) of creatures and objects.[159] What Shaman is doing, of course, is seeing optical illusions among the lines of the *greille*, projected down from the posited "dome" of Heaven onto the plane stereographic projection we considered back in Illustration 10. Latter-day shamans will refer to our stereographic projection not only as the *kátapetasma*, but as the "heavenly veil."[160] You will recall that we Celts called it the *greille*. We will not be too far afield if we visualize images of Clark Gable and Vivian Leigh, dressed as Margaret Mitchell's *Gone With The Wind* characters Rhett Butler and Scarlett O'Hara, being projected onto the silver screen of our favorite movie house. Try to hold this in your mind: a movie screen in the sky, with God Almighty as the scriptwriter, producer, director, and projectionist. No laughing, please. Shaman devoutly believes in what he is seeing.

I must pause to ask each of you to consider your personal line between reality and fantasy. Perhaps I can help your thinking by sharing with you some of my reality. We all know that Margaret Mitchell, Clarke Gable, and Vivian Leigh were more than appearances on the silver screen. (Margaret Mitchell appeared in many film news reels, you know.) Each was a human being in the flesh. Margaret Mitchell perhaps was more real to me than to you because she was my mother's friend, and we often met and talked with her in the grocery store where we shopped. How real are Rhett and Scarlett? Sometimes I must shake or pinch myself to remind myself that I met them during multiple readings of the book that once outsold the Bible, and in repeated viewings of the classical Hollywood film. Grainy patches on the celluloid of movie reels shown thousands of times kept me oriented to the fact that I was watching photographic images upon a movie screen.

But when I first viewed Ted Turner's defect-free re-release of the film, I passed over my personal line between reality and fantasy, and stood, for just a fleeting moment, face to face with my personal friends Rhett and Scarlett. My fundamentalist friends had similar experiences when they viewed their personal savior Jesus Christ on Hollywood's silver screen. Shaman saw what he saw on the stereographic projection in the sky, and was just as deeply moved.

Astronomer and Builder tried to burst Shaman's bubble, by insisting that Shaman obviously had taken more than the societally-prescribed nip of the holy plant, and had crossed over from the real world of erecting buildings aligned to the circling cosmos into the fantasy world of visions.

But Shaman was better off than our fundamentalist friends. Shaman knew he had had a vision. In Shaman's time, knowledge acquired through visions was regarded as being as real as knowledge acquired by touching one's finger to a burning ember. "Look what I have seen," Shaman told his companions, Astronomer and Builder. Shaman snatched up a stick, smoothed a place in the sand, and drew **Figures 17, 18, 19, and 20**. Shaman showed his fellow priests-scientists why and

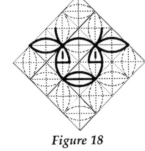

Figure 18

Figure 17

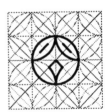

Figure 19

Figure 20

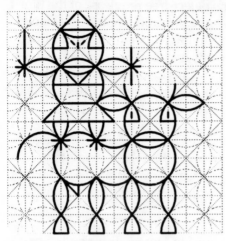

Figure 21

Illustration 15—Jupiter Dolichenus on his cosmic bull. Courtesy of Kunsthistorisches Museum, Vienna.

how he had seen the four Guardian Stars with the face of a lion, the face of an ox, the face of a man, and the face of an eagle. He showed them the likeness of a man with straight legs, hooves of a calf, two wings extended, two wings folded across the chest, and two hands under two extended wings. (Ezekiel 1:5-8, 10-11; 10:8, 14, 21-22.) Shaman named the four Guardian Stars of the Ecliptic accordingly. The others began to see images, which they shared. And, being practical men, the three priests-scientists immediately realized the value of their visions. None of them could read or write. In their society, data were encoded in stories, which stories were decoded when the data were needed. Sky stories thus became the repository for their knowledge of the apparent movements of the stars of the sky. They could not have anticipated the exegesis and hermeneusis of their stories by supposedly-learned persons of our day.

We must not fault Astronomer, Builder, and Shaman for their belief that they could acquire knowledge from the gods through the process known as "divination." Divination was as much a part of their reality as televised news programs are of ours.[161] Although the Bible expressly forbids divination, the reliance upon divination continues among some people down to our times. The Bible tells us that the Patriarch Joseph did more than drink with his cup. We are told that he also used it for divination.[162]

We have seen four examples of what Shaman saw, and a few examples of what St. Hildegard of Bingen saw millennia later. Let us conclude this segment of this paper as quickly as possible, sampling only a few images that religious seers have seen through the ages.

The bronze statuette in **Illustration 15** is of the god Jupiter-Dolichenus, known to ancient Semites as El.[163] El is the Lord-God of our Bibles; the God for whom Israel was named.[164] Will you consider whether or not this bronze image of God, cast by persons not bound by Jewish Law forbidding image-making, might have been divined from the optical illusion created in **Figure 21**, by boldfacing some of the lines of the Holy Grail?

The Grail legends tell us that Joseph of Arimathaea, who allegedly was the first priest of the Christian Church, caught in the Grail chalice the blood and water that issued forth from Christ's side after the blind centurion Longeus struck Christ with his spear.[165] As in **Figure 22**?

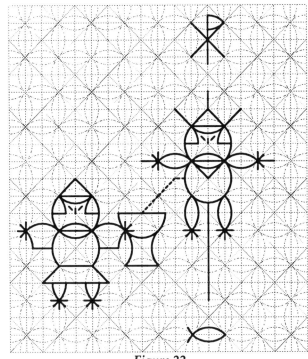

Figure 22

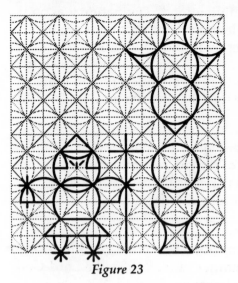

Figure 23

And what do we see in **Figure 23**? Do we see a priest with bell and crozier, summoning the Holy Spirit in the form of a dove, to convert the Host over the chalice, and the wine in the chalice, into the actual body and blood of Jesus Christ? Wolfram von Eschenbach seems to suggest that we are looking at the visionary origin of the Mass.[166]

We have seen a few examples of the Grail as plan, profile, and isometric construction drawing of the master masons, the Grail as stereographic projection of the astronomers and navigators, and the Grail as mandala of the storysmiths of religion. What, really, is the Grail, and to whom should it belong?

Literally, the Grail is our solar cosmos, the source of God's feast from Heaven. The lines we have treated as the Grail are a map of our solar system. The green silk of the Grail *achmardi* represents the green earth, and the golden threads of the Grail *achmardi* represent the rays of the sun, which fructify the soil. Grail tales allegorize the cosmic union of the sky father and the earth mother, which gives us the plants and animals that sustain human existence, i.e., the banquet from the Creator. And while Grail tales allegorize the reality of God's creation, which should belong to all of God's creatures, Grail tales also parody and satirize the modern-day *hermeneusis* (interpretation) of the Christ Story that has converted a nature cult into a system of mind-control which is used to convince the masses that the Grail belongs alone to the men and women of the power structures of church, government, and corporate enterprise.

Wolfram told a tale of a Grail knight of mixed parentage, Christian and Islamic, who was dining with the Grail king in the Grail castle.[167] In that tale, the Grail king tells the piebald knight that the Grail is the source of the food on the banquet table, which miraculously is reproduced as rapidly as it is consumed by the guests.[168] Who should be the guests at the Grail Castle? Only the elite and the effete? Or all of the creatures of God's creation, including all of humankind?

I promised you a solution to future Bosnian and Shetland wastings, but this paper soon must end. Let me redeem that promise by quoting some words of Carl Gustav Jung, who expressed his understanding of the main problem of humankind and its solution as follows: "The political and social *isms* of our day preach every conceivable ideal, but, under this mask, they pursue the goal of lowering the level of our culture by restricting or altogether inhibiting the possibilities of individual development.... This problem cannot be solved collectively, because the masses are not changed unless the individual changes.... The bettering of a general ill begins with the individual, and then only when he makes himself and not others responsible."[169]

William Blake tried to tell us that the fox condemns himself to the trap. We entrap ourselves by allowing others to think for us. We are not enslaved. We enslave ourselves. We are at fault, not our leaders. Fish swim. Birds fly. Leaders lead, but only if we let them.

The men and women of the power structures of religion, government, and commerce never will invite all of humanity to dine with them in the Grail Castle. While the rich and powerful dine around the Round Table in the Grail Castle, the rest of us continue to fight and to die in combats, the sole purpose of which are to maintain the power structures of church, government, and commercial enterprise.

Our exclusion from the Round Table in the Grail Castle will continue until enough of us realize what fools we are when the power structures divert our attention away from their theft of our birthrights by encouraging us to engage in endless disputes and combats over optical illusions visible within patterns of lines on the *greille*. For instance, nearly all of the ancients believed that the only access to Heaven was through the polar gate.[170] That "fact," like the ice dome of the sky, was a part of the "science" of their day. The only dispute was over the name of the gatekeeper at the pole star.[171] John 14:6 asserts that no one gets to God except by Jesus, i.e., Jesus is the gatekeeper. If you prefer a different interpretation for John 14:6, then consider the fact that an ancient manuscript found by Professor Morton Smith states explicitly that Jesus is the God of the pole star.[172] Our Welsh brethren previously had insisted that the gatekeeper's name was "Arthur," i.e., "awful bear,"[173] both Arthur and Jesus being references to Ursa Major, the so- called "polar guardian" or "shepherd of the circling stars."[174] While the power structures of religion, government, and commercial enterprise have dined around the Round Table in the Grail Castle, hundreds of thousands of poor dupes have died in angry combats about the name of the heavenly gatekeeper. The point was not to resolve the issue. The point was to divert the attention of the masses away from the fact that they were not allowed to dine at the Round Table of God's Grail Castle. Grail authors hoped that humankind sooner or later would wake up.[175]

As one Grail author proclaimed, let the horn be blown and the mists fade away.[176] Let humankind awake from the narcolepsy of modern-day religions. In ancient Celtic society, the entire tribe feasted from Bran's Cauldron of Plenty.[177] Let it be so among all of the tribes of humankind.

Post Scriptum

The Celtic god Bran still is around. We now call him Jesus Christ. Did you read the endnotes of this paper? The endnotes of this paper are a book within a book, and were written for the benefit of those who would like to learn more about how silly (or tragic!) it is for humankind to engage in endless religious disputes and warfare over the proper name of an optical illusion that is, at most, an avatar appearing within a pattern of lines.

𝕰𝖓𝖉𝖓𝖔𝖙𝖊𝖘

General note: References in these endnotes to "Perry" are to *The Holy Grail, Cosmos of the Bible*, ISBN: 0-8022-2557-8, by Lee Perry, published by Philosophical Library, New York, 1991, which quotes original sources as well as scholarly commentaries, is replete with endnotes, and has an extensive bibliography. My distributors are New Leaf Distributing Company, 5425 Tulane Drive, S.W., Atlanta, Georgia 30336, U.S.A., and Baker & Taylor Books, 501 South Gladiolus Street, Momence, Illinois 60954, U.S.A.

References in these endnotes to the name or names of authors (as, for instance, Messrs. Lincoln, Leigh, and Baigent) are to their works cited in the bibliography at the end of this paper.

While searching for every possible criticism of my work and my writings, Christian fundamentalists repeatedly have faulted me for citing my own book. A single moment of rational thought on their part might have opened their eyes to the need to cross reference my book and the papers I write about my book. Citations to the writings of others are provided in these endnotes, which are intended to be representative, rather than inclusive, of all sources. More extensive citations are provided in my book.

Another criticism repeatedly aimed at me is that I often cite scholarly commentaries available in inexpensive paperback books rather than the original documents closely guarded in the reserved reading rooms of important libraries worldwide. A single second of thought would reveal the reason for that practice. I have written for the benefit of the general public, as well as the scholars. Members of the general public can afford a paperback book for $9.95 from Barnes & Noble, 126 Fifth Avenue, New York, New York 10011-5666, U.S.A., but cannot afford a trip to Oxford University in England to look at an original document. Moreover, persons who are not credentialed scholars might be denied access to the original manuscript were they to make the trip!

I wish Christian fundamentalists would criticize my work on its merits, rather than taking cheap shots at me, but I suppose they no more will do that than their more warlike counterparts will stop shooting bullets and shells at each other in Bosnia-Hercegovina. After all, carpers for Christ are only a few steps removed from shooters for Christ, the distinction being one of degree rather than kind.

Please keep firmly in mind that when I offer such pungent criticisms of Christian fundamentalism, I necessarily am making fun of myself for what I believed for so many years! I cannot tease you about your beliefs because I do not have the slightest idea what they are!

Chill out, folks! The God of us all has a good sense of humor. Otherwise, how could He/She endure the worst sin of humankind, i.e., our continuing prideful ignorance? Good parents do not whack their offspring every time their children goof off or mess up. They smile, realizing that children hopefully learn from their mistakes. I am sorry for you if your God is a frowning God who belts you for every infraction. Mine tolerantly smiles down on frowners as well as smilers, and usually lets me learn things the hard way.

1. Bryant *Perlesvaus* 264-65.

2. For more details than you may be able to endure, read Oldenbourg, generally, followed by Hamilton, generally, and then finish up with Howarth, generally, and Baigent & Leigh TTATL, generally.

3. Mark 16:9; Luke 24:34. Do biblical narratives indicating that Moses and Elijah also "appeared" with Jesus (Matthew 17:3; Mark 9:4), and that Jesus' face "shone like the sun" while Jesus was on a "mountain" (Matthew 17:3), indicate that we are reading inerrant history of visionary experiences instead of inerrant history of fact? Compare Matthew 17:9 with Mark 9:9. Recall that Moses' face "shone" when he came down from "the mountain." (Exodus 34:29-30,35) The biblical phenomenon of faces that "shone" when biblical characters were on, or leaving, a "mountain," is discussed in detail in the text of this paper surrounding endnote 116.

4. Examples: Perry 201, 225-26, 239; Bryant *Perlesvaus* 27, 80- 81.

5. Examples: Genesis 15:1; Exodus 24:11; Numbers 8:4, 12:6, 24:4, 24:16; Job 33:15; Isaiah 1:1, 13:1, 21:2, 22:1, 22:5, 28:15, 28:18, 29:7,

29:11; Ezekiel 11:24, 12:24, 13:7, 43:3; Daniel 2:19, 8:1-2, 8:15-17, 8:26, 9:21, 10:14; Matthew 17:9; Acts 9:10-12, 10:3, 10:17-19, 11:5, 16:9-10, 18:9; Revelation 9:17. The Bible itself, as distinguished from some who write and preach about it, admits that many human insights about God came to seers through visions. How were those visions seen? That is the central inquiry of this paper.

6. Many people who are disinterested in church dogma nonetheless are interested in God, including me. Rejecting the preachments of the clergy, and seeking God in the mountains and deserts, may make one an apostate, but it does not make one a disbeliever. There are many ways toward God, church dogma to the contrary notwithstanding.

7. Cohen 347-386. Christian fundamentalists perusing these endnotes looking for grounds for complaint will note that Dr. Cohen's name is Jewish. I shall let Dr. Cohen speak to them in his own words: "So when I came among more intense, genuinely Bible-steeped believers than those in that liberal [Christian] church, I knew that I—and anyone else in the pertinent academic fields—really knew from nothing about the indubitable psycho-logically powerful and seemingly salutary effects to be observed in these people. I got involved, and, bereft of any intellectual resource that I thought validly refuted it, became a [Christian] believer myself. The experience, in retrospect, resembled nothing so much as a bout of substance abuse. For me, breaking out of that sticky process and gaining the insight for this book were the same event. Perhaps the experience is so little known because those who get really enmeshed in it seldom come out, or articu-late their experience if they finally do find their way out." Cohen 3. Thanks, doctor, I needed that! I am doing my best to articulate the cold shower of reality that broke *my* lifetime addiction! If you, my reader, want to come out, or are suffering because you al-ready have come out yet fear the consequences, please cure yourself by reading *The Mind of the Bible Believer*, by Dr. Edmund D. Cohen.

8. 1 Corinthians 15:13-19. Modern theologians often do not agree with Paul's all or nothing at all approach to Christianity. For instance, Father Andrew M. Greeley has suggested that the

resurrection narratives have value in modern society regardless of what a television news camera crew would, or would not, have photographed had it been present at the opening of the Tomb. Greeley 141-42. Persons often ask me where I place the line between the Jesus of history and the Christ of faith. I believe that mystery-religion elements seen as visions on the *greille*, such as the virgin birth, the transfiguration, and the resurrection, were engrafted onto the life of a real civil and religious leader, who was acting out a theurgical (as distinguished from theological) mystery play, i.e., white magic, in an attempt to bring down the ancient powers to assist the Zealots in their efforts to run the Romans off all Jewish turf. I believe your man of peace was, in reality, a man of war, and I am far from the only person who holds such views. Baigent, Leigh, and Lincoln TML 42-50.

9. A staff employee of the Society of Biblical Literature, whose name I shall not reveal lest fundamentalists mount a vendetta, wrote those words in a letter to me after reading my book *The Holy Grail, Cosmos of the Bible*. An ever-increasing number of academicians and clergy state the same opinion to me in private discussions. A few brave souls have gone public, including the Bishop of Newark, New Jersey, U.S.A., the Right Reverend John Shelby Spong. Read Spong, generally.

10. Please see the works of Messrs. Baigent, Leigh, and Lincoln, generally.

11. Your time spent reading *The Messianic Legacy* will not be wasted.

12. This mass exodus from Christianity began before my book was published. I cannot and do not claim responsibility for its beginning, which was the result of a lifetime of reading and discussion by and between Reverend J. David Davis, former pastor of the former Emmanuel Baptist Church of Athens, Tennessee, and his fellow-quester, Reverend Jack Saunders of Cleveland, Tennessee, and Cohutta, Georgia, U.S.A.

13. Details about these religious questers can be obtained by writing to Rev. J. David Davis, Emmanuel, P. O. Box 442, Athens, Tennessee 37371- 0442, U.S.A. I am not a member of their Noahide

movement. I currently am a Unitarian-Universalist, another specie of Christian "heretic" or "apostate," depending upon whether fundamentalists regard us as being inside or outside of the Christian faith. I find the open-minded peacefulness of the Noahides to be a refreshing alternative to the close-minded, warlike Southern Baptist faith in which I was steeped for most of my years. The Noahide movement rapidly has spread across the United States, and to foreign countries, at an encouraging or alarming rate, depending upon one's view of its beliefs and activities. See the bibliography after this paper for the works of Messrs. Baigent, Leigh, and Lincoln, and Professors Wilson and Mccoby, which have influenced a religious movement about which those authors probably know absolutely nothing. For alternatives to slam-dunking Christianity into the garbage can of obsolete religions, read Rev. Spong, and Frs. Fox and Greeley, whose works also are cited in the bibliography following this paper.

14. De Bhaldraithe 313. De Bhaldraithe gives us another Gaelic word corresponding to the English word "grill." He gives *branra*, a word which, if you already have read Howarth, or Baigent & Leigh TTATL, may be enough to send a cold chill shooting up your spine and to make your hair stand on end. Dinneen gives us, *inter alia*, the following meanings of *brannra*, which he spells in the ancient way, as well as in the ancient script: a support, prop, or stand; a frame on which a cake is baked; a tripod or iron rest for a pot; a pot; a gibbet.

Howarth tells us that when the Knights Templar were put to the torture after their arrests on charges, *inter alia*, of heresy, some of them confessed under torture that they had worshipped a cop-pery-colored head (Howarth 309) which, among other things, "caused the trees to flower and the land to be fertile." Howarth 280.

Baigent and Leigh guide us a few more steps up the mountain toward enlightenment by connecting the Templar "idol" with the ancient Celtic god "Bran the Blessed," whose severed head is portrayed all over your Rosslyn Chapel, who is known to you as the "Green Man" or the "Green Knight" of Grail-tale fame, and who was the ancient Celtic vegetation god or tutelary deity of fertility. Baigent & Leigh TTATL 79. There is our Gaelic word *bran* from De Bhaldraithe and Dinneen. So, we have already some evidence that the Templars were, after all, some sort of "heretics"? Probably so, but that is not the point of this inquiry.

King Robert the Bruce may have wanted you Scots to abandon Christianity in favor of ancient Celtic religion. Baigent & Leigh TTATL (18-19) tell us what Bruce sought "was nothing less than the restoration of a uniquely Celtic kingdom, with specifically Celtic institutions. These may even have included ritual human sacrifice." Anyone who thinks that going our separate tribal ways is the key to future earthly paradise should watch the evening television news! My efforts are to help you to understand the past so you can realize how absurd we are in the present, so we can avoid human conflict and environmental destruction in the future. Aldous Huxley tried to tell us that the cross borne by humankind has carved at its four extremes the words "Church," "State," "Greed," and "Hate." I do not believe in prophecy or prophesy, but those who do might wonder whether he predicted the break-up of Yugoslavia!

Please stay with me because, since childhood, I have climbed this mountain many times before! We do not have time and space in this paper for me to provide you with more than a compendium of what you would discover were you to probe deeply into ancient Irish literature. You need to understand that Irish gods presided not so much over separate phenomena, such as wind *or* rain, but over groups of phenomena. In the minds of our Celtic ancestors, Bran was the god of fertility. Thus, among other things, he caused the crops to grow. He was also the god of the bronze or iron cooking cauldron, which was suspended over the tribe's central fire by use of a tripod and chains or a metal grill. He also was god of the *axis mundi* or *stauros*, the tribal sacrificial stake, which represented, as among Native Americans, the rotational axis of our circling planet. Dinneen rarely is accused by Gaelic-speakers of not listing every meaning of a word!

Now, your flesh really is crawling. Yes, like all other white, black, yellow, and red people millennia ago, our Celtic ancestors were headhunters, human sacrificers, and human blood drinkers and flesh eaters. We still are, albeit instead of anthropophagy, i.e., eating humans who have become through "black" magic ceremonies "savior kings" when the tribe is starving to death, we now engage in theantropophagy, that is, after the Church's "white" magic, we eat the flesh and drink the blood in real presence of the Son of our God, or, if you Protestants prefer, we remember his sacrifice by eating bread and drinking wine or grape juice, in order to save ourselves not only from earthly problems, such as starvation, but to assure ourselves that we shall have life everlasting. The Church tells us that the Mass, Eucharist, or Communion is necessary for those ends, i.e., humankind cannot enjoy life and afterlife *unless* it believes and does what the Church commands. Our ancient Celtic ancestors believed in an afterlife in paradise long before the first shaman managed to convince them that only through him could they get to paradise.

Sorry, folks, this paper is short, and there is no time to mince words. (Pun intended!) I am glad we no longer actually are cannibals. I wish we would stop being symbolic cannibals. I wish we could convince ourselves that God is within us already, not doled out weekly in doses of symbolic flesh and blood, and that we need not wander mindlessly to church weekly as if we were heroin addicts going to the local clinic to get our periodic dose of methadone. If only we kick our addictions, we can be free on Sundays to wander in the woods, where we are apt to find a modern version of the Green-man avatar of the Creator God! I know. High on a mountain top is where I found my green and smiling God! I expressed my respect for Him/Her not by sacrificing some living creature (My wife finally has convinced me that I should eat vegetarian!) but by joining Green Peace and the Greens. My Ho-de-na-sau-nee (i.e., Tuscarora Tribe, Iroquoian Federation, Native American) great-grandmother surely is smiling about my "conversion." Because you do not speak her language, let me give it to you in yours: *Saoirse anois*! Béarla-speakers would say, "Freedom, now." My fellow Atlantan put it thus: "Free at last. Free at last. Thank God, I'm free at last."

I trust that I shall not be arrested under your drug laws, by which I mean your blasphemy laws, and jailed forever in some dismal dungeon for having written plain truth. I am reminded that during Patrick Henry's famous defense of a colonial publisher, when barrister Henry implored the British court to consider that his client merely had written the truth, the bumpus barrister for the Crown shouted, "The greater the truth, the greater the treason!" If your government clamps me in irons for presenting this paper, I hope that some brave Scottish dame and her Irish boatman will transport me across the western sea.

No, I am not claiming that I deserve the protection you gave your Bonnie Prince. The Scottish dame (not Dame) and her Irish boatman I had in mind were two of my maternal ancestors (The man *was* named Burke!) who made it to Culloden, Georgia, where, during the American Civil War, the Scottish woman and other women of Scottish descent mustered as a women's militia, armed primarily with hurleys and aprons full of round creek stones, to face the Yankee cavalry troop that had been sent to burn the warehouses full of grain. The menfolks were away in the regiments. The women had only one rusty cannon, which they parked in the middle of the roadway, getting the Yankees' attention. However, when the cavalry charge came, and the cannon roared once and harmlessly, it was the hurleys and stones that stopped the attack short of the warehouses, just as it was the hurleys and rocks of their menfolks which stopped the Yankee infantry's charge during a famous battle up in Virginia. The South had more stones than gunpowder. In short, I hope that if a scowling church warden comes to drag me away, the ladies and gentlemen of Scotland will hurl rocks *for* me, not *at* me! By the way, if you travel to Georgia, do not fail to see the brick warehouses in Culloden that the Yanks never burned. Ask for "Cullow-den," Georgia. We drawl, you know.

15. Currer-Briggs 28.

16. Currer-Briggs 1-4, 19-29.

17. In May of 1204, Abbot Hélinand referred to the Grail by use of the Latin words *gradalis* and *scutella lata*, which indicates that the object he had in mind was bowl-like, saucer-like, platter-like, or shield-like, and was in some way associated with a lattice. The

usual Latin word for shield is *scutum*, and its diminutive is *scutella*. The Roman shield was made of a lattice framework over which tough leather was stretched. Currer-Briggs 13, 29.

18. De Bhaldraithe 110, 164, 313; Dinneen 75.

19. Weltner 3386-87.

20. Ezekiel 1:18, 10:12.

21. Perry 4-5, 11-22, 25-32, 55-68, 71-78. If another such comparison of the verbal images of those biblical narratives with the line-form images of the *greille* exists, I have not found it, except in the tongue-in-cheek satires and parodies of those biblical verses found in the Grail-quest literature and related Celtic stories. Perry 191-283.

22. Perry 35-38, 41-53, 79-92, 98-107, 110-118, 120-123, 125131, 133-141, 145-154, 157-165, 169-186, 258-267, 271-283.

23. The optical illusion that popped into my mind was of the "Churl's Woman" from the ancient Irish satire/parody of the Christ Story known as "The Destruction of Da Derga's Hostel." The Churl's Woman is a character who has physical characteristics akin to her soul-sister, Cundrie *la sorciere*, of Grail-tale fame. Perry 207, 281-82; Cross & Slover 107; Gantz EIMAS 76; Mustard & Passage *Parzival* 169-170.

Christian fundamentalists who are able to force themselves to confront my speculations and evidence invariably state that every image from every story ever written can be found within the pattern of lines on the *greille*; hence, that I have not proven anything. I realize that I cannot prove anything to a hard- shelled fundamentalist. It is to you ladies and gentlemen that my efforts are directed.

All alligators are reptiles, but not all reptiles are alligators. A person can make up a tale linking images that he or she can find within *greille*. However, if *every* image of a tale can be found within the *greille*, then you have the first piece of evidence that the tale was written from the *greille*. Try finding *every* image of your favorite novel within the *greille*. You soon will strike out.

The second indicator that you are reading a Grail tale will be your finding the Tetramorphs, Lion, Ox, Man, and Eagle (discussed in the text of this paper between endnotes 131 and 135) among the verbal images of the story. For instance, in one Grail tale, after seeing a herdsman's **ox**, we are told that the **knight** of the spring rode up to give battle, "swifter than an **eagle**, as fierce as any **lion**," Cline 14, in response to which we learn this little memory jack:

> All four,
> Once more!
> Lion, ox,
> Man and eagle!
> We sniff them out,
> Just like a beagle! Perry 260.

Cundrie, the Churl's Woman, and similar characters provide the third indicator that we are reading a Grail tale, because *no* woman who ever lived had the physical characteristics of those two Grail womenforms, albeit *every* Grail womanform does.

Enough said about the physical characteristics of Grail womenforms, before you accuse me of gross indecency. Perry 207, 281-82. In a recent letter to Norma Lorre Goodrich, Kt. T., FSA Scot., author of *The Holy Grail*, I compared her descriptions of Cundrie (Goodrich 196-97, 217) with the classical description of the Churl's Woman (Cross & Slover 107) and exactly what I predicted would occur did occur, i.e., Mrs. Goodrich has not responded to my letter. Sorry! No offense intended! I did not make these stories up! Humankind will not progress toward enlightenment by pretending that Grail tales are something other than what they often are, i.e., bawdy, ribald romps of parody and satire making fun of Bible storysmiths and their stories, including, I am sorry to say, the Christ Story of biblical narrative. At first, these discoveries were no fun for me. I was a Christian fundamentalist, too! These discoveries hit me hard, and, unlike you, my reader, I had no one to soften the blows for me! Do wake up, please! Listen to Robert Burns, then see yourself! Learn to laugh at yourself, as I now laugh at myself! Love the God of us all, however you perceive Him/Her, and be free of the brainwashing of the power structures of church, government, and commerce.

24. Perry 205-06; Mustard & Passage *Parzival* 10, 129, 422; Gibbs & Johnson *Willehalm* 208, 292.

25. Bryant *Perceval* 143. A single wheel is seen in **Figure 2**. You should be able to find other "wheels" for yourself.

26. Bryant *Perceval* 131. A single wheel is seen in **Figure 2**. You should be able to find other "wheels" for yourself.

27. Bryant *Perceval* 149. The "flowers" are the first thing that most people see for themselves on the *greille*. One "animal" is seen in **Figure 21**. Optical illusions of other "animals," including horses, mules, bears, dogs, cats, and even squirrels, appear throughout my book.

28. Cross & Slover 93-126.

29. A magazine article recently referred to this line pattern as "one thousand and one nights," a name which is entirely appropriate, as we soon shall see in this paper. "Ireland of the Welcomes," Volume No. 41, Number 6, Nov.-Dec., 1992, page 28.

30. Currer-Briggs 204.

31. Currer-Briggs 29.

32. Encyclopaedia Britannica is a good starting place. Next, you might want to read Angus, Cumont, Godwin, Graves & Patai, Frazer, Langdon, Meyer, and many other writers on the subject. Why are those books not found in Christian book stores in the Bible-Belt where I live?

33. Try Arnheim, Frazer, Godwin, Mccoby, Sheehan, and Wilson for openers. Start with Wilson. Those books also are conspicuously

absent from Christian bookstores in my little corner of the world. Is someone hiding something that he or she knows but most folks do not know?

34. *The Compact Edition of the Oxford English Dictionary*, 1971, Vol. 1, at page 779, under the entry "*Docetae*." Perry 164-65, 191-94.

35. Hamilton 60-81; Perry 191-92; Oldenbourg, generally.

36. Perry 3, 191-95, 238, 247; Roberts 50; Partner 65, 90, 167- 68; Baigent, Leigh, and Lincoln HBHG, generally; Baigent & Leigh TTATL, generally; Oldenbourg, generally; Howarth, generally.

37. Evans THHOTHG 82; Perry 3, 200.

38. Partner 90.

39. Partner 168. One commentator (Weston) opined: "Templar knowledge of Grail secrets made them [the Knights Templar] into no ordinary heretics but into possessors of a doctrine which criticized Christianity in such a fundamental and radical way that at the time of the Templar trial the existence of the Grail heresy had to be hushed up, so as not to imperil the very survival of the Christian faith." Partner 168.

40. Oldenbourg 359-62.

41. Baigent & Leigh TTATL 51-53, 63-76.

42. Baigent & Leigh TTATL 34-37, 76; Sinclair 46-47. I recommend that you read Andrew Sinclair's *The Shroud and the Grail*, if you are interested in the many contributions of his illustrious family to Scottish history. I am amused rather than angered that, after his having acknowledged by postcard his receipt of a copy of my book, *The Holy Grail, Cosmos of the Bible*, several months before the publication of his book, he declared in his book, *ex cathedra*, that a relationship between "grail" and "grille" is "unlikely." Sinclair 64. Perhaps he did not read my book, or his Gaelic is worse than mine, or he did not want to join me in apostasy, or, having read

my book, he simply does not agree with me. (Please refer back to our earlier discussion of *greille* and *grátáil* in the text of this paper before endnotes 14 and 31.) I mean to give him all respect that he is due as a descendant of your former lords of these isles.

Some English, apparently being thoroughly brainwashed by the Church, prefer to accept as whole truth the comic spectacle of their grand army's running away during the Battle of Bannockburn when, as the Church-sponsored fable goes, they were confronted by a motley crew of Scottish butchers, bakers, and candlestick makers. That avoids candidly admitting that their brave soldiers wisely advanced to the rear when Knights Templar, carrying the *gonfalon baucent*, i.e., the Templar battle standard or flag (Howarth 57-58), and shouting the Templar battle cry *"Baucent"* (Howarth 59), suddenly came charging across the field. To understand the reality of such an assault by Templar knights, recall what happened to entire regiments of Iraqi foot soldiers who found themselves confronting our heavy battle tanks during the recent exchange of unpleasantries near the Persian Gulf. Why does the Church want to pretend that *real* Templars in significant numbers never existed in Scotland? Because the claims of modern-day Scottish speculative freemasons that they *actually* are the inheritors of the Templar traditions might gain widespread acceptance if people knew that *real* Templars had been out and about in the Highlands! Bakers of haggis? Or, Templar knights? As you like it!

43. Baigent & Leigh TTATL 64-76, 111-122; Sinclair, generally.

44. Oldenbourg 359-62. Bishop Bertrand Marty, a Cathar bishop who soon would be burned at the stake, gave Pierre-Roger, *inter alia*, "a piece of green cloth." Oldenbourg 359.

45. See all three of those names in the bibliography following this paper. Their writings are many, and right to the point of what this paper is all about.

46. Hozeski 129.

47. Hozeski 141. Hildegard is referring to the mystery of the Mass, which she saw in her sky visions; hence, understood. Hozeski 129, 141. At endnote 166 of this paper, we shall see for ourselves what Hildegard probably saw.

48. Hozeski and Fox, generally. 2 Fox 22, in particular.

49. Perry 196; Mustard & Passage 244.

50. Hozeski 4.

51. Perry 257; 1 Fox 7, 16, 48, 80-81.

52. Perry 257; Hozeski 41, 83.

53. Perry 69, 318; Allen ix, 26; Farbridge 132-33, 171; Wisdom of Solomon 13:1-9.

54. Perry 70, 318; Graham 354. Graham quotes from Thomas Jefferson, as follows: "'The day will come,' said he, 'when the mystical generation of Jesus by the supreme being as his father in the womb of a virgin will be classed with the fable of the generation of Minerva in the brain of Jupiter.'" Graham 304. In my book, I quoted further from Jefferson, as follows: "'Man is fed with fables through life, leaves it in the belief he knows something of what has been passing, when in truth he has known nothing but what has passed under his own eye.'" Perry 5; Malone 106; from a letter by Thomas Jefferson to Thomas Cooper, dated December 11, 1823. One of America's founding fathers apparently was less a true believer than modern Christian fundamentalists would prefer to believe.

55. Perry 69-70; Dobin 139.

56. Hozeski 7-8.

57. Perry 257; 2 Fox 22.

58. Perry 257; 1 Fox 52; 2 Fox 308.

---

59. Perry 158; Williamson 44.

60. Perry 159; Minnaert 290-95.

61. Perry 257; Hozeski 2. Hildegard was not alone in suggesting that the Bible must be read allegorically. Saint Augustine was of the opinion that "[I]gnorance of number prevents us from understanding things that are set down in the scripture in a figurative and mystical way." Perry 198, 318; James 85.

R.A. Schwaller de Lubicz wrote of the Christian Gospels: "The purpose of these parables and enigmatical phrases is not to hide anything from 'he who has eyes to see and ears to hear,' according to the evangelical formula. The purpose is to select those who have developed the necessary understanding and who are for this reason worthy of those 'secrets' (that is to say, they will not misuse them for selfish motives). There was never any intent to conceal, from those thus prepared, any of the wisdom transmitted by texts, traditions, or monuments. The enigma does not lie in the thing itself but is the result of our understanding, our faculties, and our intelligence, which are not attuned to the mentality according to which the idea was expressed, and it is just this that our present education prevents us from admitting." Perry 287; Schwaller de Lubicz 1617.

Eusebius of Caesarea, 263-339 C.E., who sat beside and supported Emperor Constantine during the Council of Nicaea, 325 C.E., during which the Roman specie of Christianity was founded, later wrote the first history of the Roman Church, in which he expressed the opinion that the *Therapeutae* described by Claudius Philo were a source of the syncretic faith that later became known as "Christianity." Eusebius tells us that what Philo had referred to as the "short works" of those religionists "were the gospels, the apostolic writings, and in all probability passages interpreting the old prophets, such as are contained in the Epistle to the Hebrews and several others of Paul's epistles." Perry 160; Eusebius 91. Eusebius tells us that Philo wrote of those religionists that "'Their explanations of the sacred scriptures are expressed figuratively in allegories. For the whole Law seems to them to resemble a living being, which for body has the literal precepts, for soul the mean-

ing that is hidden in the words out of sight.'" Perry 161; Eusebius
93.

The Church Triumphant despised its founding father and first
historian, Eusebius of Caesarea, and modern-day theologians
usually deprecate his writings, saying that his Greek was of the
streets rather than the seminaries, and his ideas were proletarian
rather than patrician. After my presentation last year of a paper
about my work, during the 27th International Congress on
Medieval Studies, at Kalamazoo, Michigan, a scowling and
almost-shouting brother of a certain Roman Catholic order,
threatened me with the fires of eternal Hell for having suggested
that some biblical verses are inerrant history of visionary experiences instead of being inerrant history of fact. When I reminded
him about what Eusebius had written respecting biblical allegory,
the scowl intensified and the decibels doubled, and his spittle
sprayed my face as he fulminated against Eusebius. Fortunately
for me, burnings at the stake for apostasy no longer are legal
anywhere in the United States! Brother Whatever-his-name
balled up his fist as if to strike me with knuckles as well as
sprayed spittle. Fortunately for him, his outburst cooled his
emotions and he did not strike a blow for his faith. Despite severe
osteoarthritis and declining eyesight, I still can employ effectively
my Army Ranger training!

62. Hozeski xi.

63. Lorayne & Lucas 83-93.

64. See endnote 32.

65. See endnote 33.

66. Aveni 26, 84-85, 92-93; Brown 214-225; Hadingham 186-203;
     Krupp 306.

67. The Planet Venus, the "Queen of Heaven," has been known by
     many names through the years, including Inanna, Is(h)tar, Usas,
     Isis, and Mary. Perry 363 will lead readers to many sources of sky
     stories about the "Queen of Heaven."

68. Perry 151; Budge 2 Osiris 281.

69. Perry 164; Langdon TBEOC 16, 20-33, 58-59; 1 Frazer 109- 120, 178-79, 213-253.

70. Eisenman & Wise, generally.

71. *The Dead Sea Scrolls Deception.* See bibliography.

72. Oxford 1186; Currer-Briggs 1-29; Goodrich, generally; Sinclair 63-88. Baigent and Leigh still insist that "Grail" is a reference to *sang réal*, i.e., the royal blood. Baigent & Leigh TTATL 78.

   Having correctly associated "Grail" with *greille*, Currer- Briggs speculates that the Grail was a grillwork casket in which the Shroud or Sindon was kept. Currer-Briggs 29, 67.

   Sinclair expresses the view that the Grail "is the quest for God's grace"; hence, that "It cannot be reached, only sought." Sinclair 88.

   Goodrich gives us an excellent overview of the many speculations about the Grail (Goodrich, generally) and she even realizes that the Grail is "en samblance de calice." Goodrich 157. Contrary to Sinclair, the Grail stories, themselves, indicate that the Grail is something upon which images appear then disappear. Perry 225, 247; Bryant *Perlesvaus* 26, 195-96. And, as Goodrich acknowledges, one of those images has the appearance of a chalice. Goodrich 157; Perry 247; Bryant *Perlesvaus* 195-96.

73. Perry 205-06 brings together the references to the Grail as being an *achmardi*, i.e., a piece of precious green silk upon which a pattern of lines was sewn in gold threads. Do you remember the "green cloth" that was brought down from Montségur, and spirited away into hiding? Endnote 44. If you want to read about the Grail *achmardi* in English-language translations of the original tale, refer to Mustard & Passage 10, 129; *and* Gibbs & Johnson 208, 292.

Perry 18-19, 202, and Mustard & Passage 128, 252, will give you references to the Grail as a thin stone "so clear that in the day the sun shone through." In an effort to save space in these endnotes, let me summarize where in my book you can find Ezekiel's and the Mayans' green stone centering the heavens, King Athelstan's crystal in which one can see the "True Cross," and a black-and-white photograph of what everyone was writing about. Perry 18-19, 22, 114, 184, 202, 257, 259, 330. Ah ha, shriek the fundamentalists, Perry has failed again to cite to the originals and, *ergo*, he is no scholar! Answer: Go where I have sent you and see what you find! My book is replete with citations to the originals!

74. Perry 292. The four classical vaults. By permission. From *Webster's Third New International Dictionary* © 1986, at page 2536, by Merriam-Webster, Inc., publisher of the Merriam-Webster® dictionaries.

75. Perry 18. Courtesy of Dover Publications, Inc., New York. Perry 45. Courtesy of Ms. Doreen Yarwood and Bounty Books, London.

76. Perry 298-300. Ghyka 16 is but one example.

77. Perry 303-06. James, generally.

78. Perry 294-95. Examples are to be found in Gimpel 74, 85.

79. We are not talking about modern-day science, which often begins in the mind of a mathematician, then goes to the desk of a pure scientist, after which it is translated into bits and bytes by a computer programmer, and then into the CAD-CAM drawing of a process engineer. The end result might be a "boom-box" radio to blast rap music into our ears! We are talking, instead, about empirical science of a primitive but effective sort, which works like this: To know and to please God, and to build things as well as He did, you first look at what God has made, then you copy it, because if it worked for God, it just might work for you. The end results were Gothic cathedrals that have stood for centuries! Perry 297-300.

80. While John James was "decoding" Chartres Cathedral, he discovered that a master mason had taken his crystallography so far as to bend deliberately the axes of the cathedral to replicate the phenomenon known as "dislocation," which appears in quartz and other crystals. That planning and construction would have been no practical value to his clients, the clergy, and would not have strengthened the cathedral construct. Apparently, it was done that way because God makes crystals that way, and for no other reason! Perry 306; James 103-04. Unlike earlier Greek temples, that contained architectural tricks to please the human eye, the Gothic cathedral was built to replicate on Earth God's home in the sky, imitation being the sincerest form of flattery! Perry 303; James 147.

81. Please refer to **Illustration 10** of this paper.

82. I hasten to add that we are talking about mathematical crystallography, not about the hocus-pocus crystallomancy of which New Age religionists are so fond.

83. Please refer to **Illustration 10** of this paper, and to the pages of this paper immediately following that illustration.

84. Perry 18. Courtesy of Dover Publications, New York.

85. Perry 19. Muireachdach's Cross, Monasterboice, County Louth, Ireland. Courtesy of the Office of Public Works, Republic of Ireland.

86. **Illustrations 1 & 7** appear, respectively, in Perry 4, 295, by courtesy of the British Museum, London.

87. Perry 295; Gimpel 74. Courtesy of Michael Russell (Publishing) Ltd, Wilton, Salisbury, England. I was privileged to meet Messr. Jean Gimpel during the 27th International Congress of Medieval Studies, May 7-10, 1992, at Kalamazoo, Michigan, U.S.A., during which I presented a paper to The International Society of Hildegard von Bingen Studies, of which I am a member. Messr. Gimpel, a scholar of considerable wit as well as knowledge, was pleased to learn that at least one Babylonian scribal student of

1800-1600 B.C.E. was as familiar with the construct for "doubling the square" as was the master mason of European cathedrals, Villard de Honnecourt. Scholars, the clergy, and lay persons of the working poor and middle classes tend to react favorably to my work. Rich or powerful representatives of government, business, the Church's hierarchy, and the news media tend to react negatively. Why? Perhaps they do not want the citizenry to think for themselves?

88. Perry 294-96. The *real* scholar to whom I refer on page 296 of my book is Messr. Jean Gimpel. Gimpel 85-86.

89. Perry 294; Gimpel 85.

90. Perry 296; Gimpel 85-86.

91. Perry 300; 1 Heath 160.

92. Perry 300; Lawlor 96-97.

93. Perry 295; Gillings 1; Neugebauer 35-36.

94. Perry 300, 303; James 83, 147.

95. Perry 15; Ezekiel 1:22-23; Oxford Study Edition of the New English Bible with the Apocrypha 887 fns.

96. Oxford, ibid. The ancient Hebrews believed that when God was on the job, He sat "throned on the vaulted roof of the earth," (Isaiah 40:22, New English Bible) and that when he traveled about He "rode on a cherub... [and] flew through the air." (2 Samuel 22:11, New English Bible) They also believed that God communed with them and delivered to them His commands while He was seated between the two cherubim on the lid of the Ark of the Covenant (Exodus 25:21-22), which ancient cosmology apparently was too much for the Prophet Jeremiah, who longed for the day when the Hebrews would slam dunk such cosmic concepts into the trash can of obsolete religion. Jeremiah predicted that the day would come when "men shall speak no more of the Ark of

the Covenant of the Lord; they shall not think of it nor remember it nor resort to it; it will be needed no more." (Jeremiah 3:16, New English Bible) Jeremiah hoped that the cosmic concept of the "Queen of Heaven" would suffer a similar fate (Jeremiah 7:18; 44:17-19, 25) but, instead, the Church promoted Our Lady to the job! Perry 363 "Queen of Heaven" will give you a rather complete overview of that royal succession.

97. Oxford, ibid.

98. Perry 8; Frankfort 31-61, 125-84, 223-54.

99. Perry 75-76; 1 Kings 7:23.

100. Perry 63. Exodus 25:31-37 calls for twenty-two cups or bowls upon which seven lamps are to sit. Scholars say the "lampstand" is an allegory for the sun, the moon, and the five visible planets— Mercury, Venus, Mars, Jupiter, and Saturn. Perry 63; Cirlot 257-59, 283-85; Graves & Patai 13, 25, 52-53.

101. Because the scriptures state explicitly that the plans and specifications for the Tabernacle (Exodus 25:8-9) and for the Temple (1 Chronicles 28:11-19; Wisdom of Solomon 9:8) were drafted by God, and that the Israelites had to follow those plans and specifications without variance if they wanted God to dwell among them on Earth, it necessarily followed that innovative Hebrew mathematicians could not be allowed by the priestly classes to insist, openly, that 3.14 is the correct value, thereby contradicting God's decree that the correct value is 3.0! 1 Kings 7:23. During the Middle Ages, the Church still insisted that the sky is a "tent," i.e., a tabernacle. Dreyer 211.

102. Perry 297-98; Ghyka 21, 113, 116; 1 Heath 69-74.

103. Beckmann 174-77. St. Augustine was of the opinion that "[I]gnorance of number prevents us from understanding things that are set down in the scripture in a figurative and mystical way." Perry 298, 318; James 85. Perhaps, I will not be faulted for suggesting that persons who are numerate as well as literate will appreciate what the mathematics of probability suggests about

several hundred serial matches between verbal images and line-form images, as analyzed in my book, i.e., a margin of error very closely approaching zero.

104. Perry 11.

105. Deuteronomy 18:10; Exodus 22:18.

106. Baigent & Leigh TTATL 111-122.

107. Perry 318-329; Hapgood, generally.

108. Perry 344-45; Nissen 34-39; Deacon 129-176.

109. Perry 317-47.

110. Perry 319. Courtesy of Dover Publications, Inc., New York.

111. Perry 319; Hapgood 212.

112. Perry 319; Hapgood 17, 23, 27, 30, 36, 43, 46, 98, 102-04, 110, 115, 140.

113. Perry 85; Kramer 302, 304. Courtesy of the University of Chicago Press.

114. Perry 85; Kramer 302, 304. Courtesy of the University of Chicago Press.

115. Perry 85; Kramer 302, 304. Courtesy of the University of Chicago Press.

116. Perry 86; Exodus 34:29-30, 35.

117. Perry 93, 328-29; Krupp 129, 131, 133, 138, 140-41, 317-18, 322; Hadingham 152-56. Compare Newgrange in Ireland. Perry 313; Wood 80-81; McMann 24-25; Service & Bradbery 41, 144; Brennan 7- 126. Please recall that these endnotes are not intended to be comprehensive of the many available sources.

118. Perry 347; Ezekiel 1:16-17.

119. Perry 340-41; Lawrence 38. Courtesy of Dover Publications, Inc., New York.

120. Perry 309; Fanning 20-24; Dreyer 305, 308, 328, 392-93; 416- 17, Heath *Aristarchus* 141-143; Washburn 7.

121. The writing on our Babylonian tablets reads, "A square, the side is 1. Inside it are 4 quadrants and 16 boat-shapes. I have drawn 5 regular concave-sided tetragons. This area, what is it?" Perry 7; Oates 185; Saggs 453.

122. Perry 340; Heafford 104.

123. Perry 340; Heafford 104.

124. Perry 340; Heafford 104.

125. Perry 341; Lawrence 38.

126. Perry 340; Dreyer 389.

127. Perry 339; Hoyle 105, 121; Wood 75; Brown 119.

128. Perry 340; Wood 40-50.

129. Perry 346; Ezekiel 1:16-17.

130. Perry 93; Dreyer 310-11. Kepler's mother was tried by the Church for witchcraft in 1620. The records of the trial are extant. Robbins 544. Galileo was tried by the Church and threatened with the death penalty if he did not recant his theories of astronomy. Dreyer 416.

131. Perry 1, 3, 11-22, 25, 35, 65, 91, 95, 102, 117, 152, 260, 281, 317-18; Allen ix, 26, 255-56, 344-46, 360-62, 366, 378, 381- 82, 385; Rey 50, 52, 56, 130-36, 139.

132. Perry 317; Allen 256.

133. Perry & Allen, endnote 131.

134. Ezekiel 1:5, 10; 10:14,15,22; Cirlot 337-39.

135. Perry 95; Cirlot 337-39.

136. Perry 95, 317-18; Allen, endnote 131.

137. Perry 317; Allen 378.

138. Perry 317; Allen 256.

139. Perry 2, 84, 93, 129; Dreyer 310-11, 416.

140. Is that not what you were taught in school?

141. Perry 308-09; Heath *Aristarchus* 301.

142. Perry 93; Robbins 544.

143. Perry 310-12; Dreyer 207-239.

144. Perry 310; Ronan 7-8; Hapgood 190-91.

145. If you do not see within the pages of this paper evidence sufficient to allow you to reach that conclusion, then read my book.

146. Perry 310; Ronan 8; Hapgood 190-91; Dreyer 206.

147. Endnote 139.

148. Hamilton 60-81.

149. Oldenbourg 340-64. On March 16, 1244, the church burned to
death at the foot of Montségur over 200 Cathars.

150. Perry 192; Oldenbourg 28-81; Brooke 100-01.

151. Ibid.

152. Ibid.

153. Ibid.

154. Perry 310; Dreyer 206; 2 Heath GM 453, 519, 528-29.

155. Perry 336-39. The early Sumerian "star" we considered at endnote 113 appears at Stonehenge, either by coincidence or design, as a diagram limiting the directions of sunrise and sunset, moonrise and moonset, during the progression of each year. Perry 339; Wood 9-10.

156. "Bishop Spong: 'I'm a seeker of the truth,'" an article appearing on the religion page of the Saturday, December 12, 1992, edition of The Atlanta Journal-Constitution.

157. Modern city-dwellers will have a hard time believing that the stars could light the work of our three desert-dwellers. Some things must be seen to be believed!

158. Perry 134-35, 147, 154, 163, 266, 269, 333.

159. Perry 193-94; Walker 34-35.

160. The New English Bible tells us (Acts 10:10-12, 16) that Peter "... fell into a trance. He saw a rift in the sky, and a thing coming down that looked like a great sheet of sail-cloth. It was slung by the four corners, and was being lowered to the ground. In it he saw creatures of every kind, whatever walks or crawls or flies." We are assured that after certain verbal instructions to Peter from God, "the thing was taken up again into the sky."

Please recall the concave-sided tetragon we saw in **Figure 1**, which fits that description precisely. Please also recall that the greille is decorated with animals. See the text of this paper at endnote 27, and Perry 53. Accordingly, will you permit yourself to agree with me that the Bible, itself, refers to the greille?

The Temple, being an earthly version of its heavenly counterpart, also had a veil. Perry 67; Exodus 26:31-37. The Letter of Aristeas, a Christian writing outside of the Canon of the Bible, has quite a lot to say about the veil of the Temple, and its resemblance to the wind-filled mainsail of a square-rigged sailing ship. Perry 53; Aristeas 4:8-9.

In a Norse legend, we are told that the great ship of the gods, Skithblathnir or Skidbladnir, which is large enough for all of the gods and their equipment, "[M]ay be laid together like a cloth and put in one's pocket." Perry 195, 210; Hollander 62; Crossly-Holland 51. Why not if, as we suspect, the great ship of the gods appears on the *Katapetasma*, the *greille achmardi*, or the Heavenly Veil! In another Germanic saga, we are told that Thor's mighty "hammer," Mjollnir, can be folded up like a cloth and tucked inside your shirt. Crossly-Holland 52. It is difficult to avoid the humor implicit in those representations.

Goodrich tells us that she is much perplexed by the tale in which Joseph of Arimathaea and 150 companions sail to Britain on a *linea*, that is, on a linen, sail, canvas, or shirt. She concludes that the storysmith is employing a figure of speech, a rhetorical device known as *synecdoche*, that is, the author is referring to the whole, a ship, by reference to one of its parts, a sailcloth. Goodrich 78-81. I wrote her about the great ship of the Norse gods, which can be folded away like your hanky, but she did not respond. Good Christians cannot permit themselves to see these tales for what they are: satires and parodies upon the official *hermeneusis* (inter-pretation) of the Christ Story that was put into the minds of our European ancestors by the Albigensian Crusade and the Inquisi-tions! Believe as the Church says, or die! Goodrich concludes that "it is uncanny how these Grail texts imitate the Old Testa-ment...." Goodrich 81. She got that one right!

The Bible tells us that Moses wore a veil over his face when his face shone. (Exodus 34:33-35) As with great ships that can be folded like a handkerchief and put into your pocket, the Grail-tale authors generated endless parody and satire about Grailform persons with cloths covering the faces. For instance, our presum-ably-Templar author of *Perlesvaus* told a tale of a maiden who found on an altar a piece of the cloth that covered the body of Christ, but that when she reached out, "...it rose into the air as though a wind had seized it, and hung so high above an ancient crucifix there in the chapel that she could not reach it." Perry 242-43; Bryant *Perlesvaus* 143-46. Did members of the power structures for whom Grail tales were performed by naughty minstrels listen to such entertainments with sanctified, beatified smiles on their faces? Or, did they smile knowingly, then laugh out loud?

We are told, quite solemnly, that when Jesus died, the curtain (i.e., the veil) of the temple was torn in two from top to bottom. Matthew 27:51; Mark 15:38; Luke 23:45. Visionary cosmology that has become faith? Or, fact? By the way, my New English Bible has the centurion deliver this one-liner when Jesus died: "Truly, this man was *a* son of God." (Emphasis added.) Mark 15:39. Correct translations often vaporize modern dogmas. My New English Bible also indicates that God, not Jesus, selects those humans who are raised up to Heaven "on the last day" (John 6:44); that "all who are moved by the Spirit of God are sons of God" (Romans 8:14); and that Jesus claimed to be a son of God only in the sense that we all are. John 10: 31-36. I wear proudly my badges of "apostate" and "heretic," which means that I refuse to swallow the stuff the Church hands out, but do not accuse me of disbelief in a God of us all.

This is my favorite joke about God: Billy Bob and Tommy Joe, two Georgia "rednecks" dressed in bed sheets and pointed hoods, were helping their fellow members of the KKK to lynch an African-American who had failed to say "Yes, sir" to the Klan's illustrious leader, the local manufacturer of illegal alcohol. Up drove two deputy sheriffs. In the exchange of gunfire, Billy Bob and Tommy Joe were killed. Saint Peter opened the Golden Gates, issued them sets of wings, and they took their places in a long line of new arrivals waiting to go before the Throne of God. Billy Bob went first, then came out to tell Tommy Joe the good news and the bad news. The good news was that they had made it into Heaven, and Tommy Joe soon would meet God. The bad news was that She's black. How do you know She isn't? My God has a good sense of humor. I feel sorry for you if yours doesn't.

161. Perry 12; Oates 178-80.

162. Perry 12; Genesis 44:5. The Bible forbids divination (Deuteronomy 18:10) but getting all of the biblical Hebrews to give up divination would be as formidable a task as getting every modern Scot to give up *uisce beatha*!

163. Perry 138-39, 142; Godwin 154; Langdon TMOAR 37-45.

164. Langdon TMOAR 37-45; Graves & Patai 229.

165. Perry 181. The Norse cried for Balder like the Hebrews and their Semitic Babylonian cousins cried for Tammuz. (Davidson 21, 36, 110, 184; Branston 145-47, 157, 161; Ezekiel 8:14) In the Norse sagas, Balder was killed by the blind god, Hoder, using a spear made of mistletoe fashioned by the Trickster, Loki (Davidson 35, 36, 187; Branston 158-59), much as Christ reputedly expired by the lance thrust of Longeus, a Roman centurion, whose blindness reputedly was cured by the effusion of blood and water from Christ's side (Branston 169: John 19:34), provided, of course, you can imagine a blind Roman centurion's being on military duty at all, much less officiating at such an important event as the crucifixion of Jesus. I presume that you cosmologists know the in-the-Bible and out-of-the-Bible versions of these stories better than do I.

   Although the stereotyped, modern depiction of Christ on the Cross illustrates both feet nailed to the upright post with a single spike, the very earliest depictions of the crucifixion show Him, arms extended to a horizontal beam, *legs straight down*, either sitting or standing on a lower horizontal beam. Smith 61- 62; Perry 33. Our Grail manform can be visualized either sitting or standing on a lower horizontal beam. Bold the lines for yourself!

166. Perry 197-99; Mustard & Passage 252.

167. Perry 205-06; Mustard & Passage 421-22.

168. Ibid.

---

169. Perry 169; Jung 65.

170. Perry 37-38, 95, 140, 322-24. "[T]his rock, and this gate, are the Son of God." 3 Hermas 9:109. "All of the ancient world looked upon the polar center as the 'middle place,' 'resting place,' or 'steadfast region' occupied by the Universal Monarch." Talbott 42. "Wearing a jewelled crown... [the polestar] stands before Abathur's door at the gate of the world of light; the Mandaeans [St. John Christians or Nasoraeans] invariably pray with their faces turned northward." Allen 456. The Holy Koran tolerates "Sabians" (Baptists), i.e., the St. John Christians. Sura II.62. Dozens of pages of text and citations in my book cannot be compressed into this brief endnote, which surely will lead Christian fundamentalists to scream, "Perry admits that his new paper is incomplete!" They would not read my first book because it was too long and expensive, and will not read this one because it is too short. I understand. So do you.

171. The cosmic gatekeeper or herdsman of the rotating stars has been known by many names. "Santa Claus, descending yearly from his polar home to distribute gifts around the world, is a muffled echo of the Universal Monarch, the primordial Osiris, Yama, or Kronos spreading miraculous good fortune.... The home of the great father is the cosmic center—the 'heart,' 'midst,' or 'navel' of heaven." Talbott 42; Perry 322.

Meister Eckhart, 1260-1329, C.E., a German Dominican whose roots were in the nature-oriented, Celtic tradition of spirituality, rather than the fall-redemption-oriented Christianity of Rome, served as vicar-general of the Irish monastic foundation at Ratisbon (Regensburg) in Germany. Fox *Breakthrough* 1, 30-34.

Meister Eckhart expressed these views about Heaven: "Heaven runs constantly in a circle.... [I]t bestows on all creatures their beings and their lives.... Heaven does not have this power of itself but rather from an angel who causes it to revolve. As I have also often said, all the 'images' and preliminary images or 'ideas' of all of the creatures were already created by the angels before they were created corporeally in creatures....[B]y causing heaven to revolve, the angel pours out all of the first images of creation which he has received from God...." Fox *Breakthrough* 367-68. Is Meister Eckhart describing the *Katapetasma* as source of the *Paradeigmata*? (See text at endnote 160.) Eckhart also stated, "As a result of heaven's rotation, everything in the world flourishes and bursts into leaf." Fox *Breakthrough* 120. We moderns know that Planet Earth's rotation around the Ecliptic gives us the seasons, which causes everything in the world to flourish and burst into leaf. Eckhart apparently knew about Ezekiel's wheel within a wheel, and its consequences!

About humans' questing for God, Eckhart said, "[T]he soul can find no rest until it understands God, insofar as it is possible for a creature to understand God." Fox *Breakthrough* 366. Eckhart says that in its quest for God, the human spirit "storms the firmament and scales the heavens until it reaches the Spirit that drives the heavens.... [I]t presses on ever further into the vortex" of the "circle of being of which the Creator is the center point." Fox *Breakthrough* 95-96, 354-55. See Perry 195 for these references to Meister Eckhart.

Grail questers should feel at home in the pages of *Popol Vuh*, one of a handful of Mayan cosmology codexes that escaped the bonfires of ardent, Christian missionaries. Tedlock 27. We are told by the Mayan authors of *Popol Vuh* how "Heart of Sky," an anthropomorphic, one-legged, trinitarian god, created human-kind and the world of light. Tedlock 73, 343. Polar guardians often are described as one-legged. Perry 264, 277.

We are told that the Mayan icon for the Planet Venus is a severed head. Tedlock 236. Do you remember what we learned in endnote 14 about the severed head of the Celtic god, Bran?

The Mayan authors of the *Popol Vuh* tell us that their council book is "a place to see 'The Light That Came from Across the Sea.'" Tedlock 71. Is this a reference to Jesus Christ or to the Spanish Roman Catholic missionaries? Christian fundamentalists may spring for such a conclusion, but cosmologists surely realize that what I am about to summarize probably came from some source other than a devout Christian missionary!

Tedlock comments that the Mayan words he translates as "a place to see" refer to "an instrument (or place) for the seeing of something," and that the something to be seen "could variously mean 'figure,' 'drawing,' and even 'picture.'" Tedlock 242-43. Tedlock says that one of those Mayan words would refer today "to crystals used for gazing by diviners and to eyeglasses, binoculars, and telescopes." Tedlock 243. Ezekiel's sapphire crystal appears right in middle of the Holy Grail! Perry 22; Ezekiel 1:26. Did the Mayans know about the Holy Grail? If so, how? Or, is it merely a coincidence that *Popol Vuh* contains so many elements of Grail tales?

Tedlock refers to another Mayan codex which indicates that "Heart of Sky" or "Heart of Heaven" is a "bead of precious stone." Tedlock 254. Ezekiel would have agreed! Ezekiel 1:26.

The Mayan gods-heroes of *Popol Vuh* engaged in form-changing; and they spend days in ritual combats, and nights in a variety of perilous "houses" and "citadels," including the citadel of the bearded place! Tedlock 43-45, 55-56, 137-150. If this cosmology came to the Mayans from some Spanish priest, he apparently had a copy of *Perlesvaus* hidden under his cassock! Perry 212-250.

Popol Vuh tells us that the Mayan gods are sustained by "the ultimate fruits of the earth and sky, which were themselves described as the 'blue-green plate' and the 'blue-green bowl.'" Tedlock 58. The Grail *achmardi*? See the text of this paper at endnotes 72 and 73, and the contents of endnote 73. Do not expect me to tell you the source of this Mayan cosmology. I do not know!

Those references to *Popol Vuh* may be found in Perry 330.

172. Perry 186; Smith 63.

173. *Arth uthr* are the *Cymraeg* (Welsh) words for "bear-awful." Evans *Dictionary* 43, 253. The association between King Arthur and the constellation Ursa Major, the Great Bear, has been noted by commentators. Baigent, Leigh, and Lincoln HBHG 239; Matthews 342-48. The so-called "Mithras Liturgy" refers to "the

Bear which moves and turns heaven around, moving upward and downward in accordance with the hour." Meyer 218. The Phrygians spoke of the cosmic goatherd Aipolos, he who "rotates the whole universe in a circle." Meyer 151. Meister Eckhart said that an angel causes heaven to revolve. Fox *Breakthrough* 367-68. The Desana Indians of Colombia determine the arrival and departure of the seasons by the stars, in connection with which they tell a sky story about the Master of the Animals (Perry 327; Krupp 319), a supernatural gamekeeper, whose role in the Cosmos parallels that of the Grail giant who herds the constellations of stars in a tale from the Welsh *Mabinogion* (Perry 264-65; Gantz *Mabinogion* 196-97), and in the writings of Chrétien de Troyes. Perry 258; Cline 8-9. The Irish god Lug and the Germanic god Odin also appeared as limping polar guardians. Perry 264; Gantz *Mabinogion* 196-97. Like other polar guardians, King Arthur limped. Guest 271. Eastern Christian tradition says Christ was lame, as well as red-headed (Perry 259; Tribbe 221, 246), which leads us to recall red-headed and lame Thor. (Perry 175, 259; Cavendish 181) Our little humanform on the Holy Grail justly has been called "the being with many names." Meyer 153. The great mythologist Joseph Campbell tried to tell us these things when he wrote about the Hero with a Thousand Faces.

174. Readers who are tired of what may appear to be useless sky stories perhaps will be less bored when they become aware of the fact that our little *greille* manform, in his role as the locator of the star *Kochab*, was used by ancient sailors in the Northern Hemisphere to calculate longitude, and still is used by modern sailors who seek verification that their electronic navigational equipment is functioning properly! Perry 201; Morison 154.

So many people think of Arthur as a real king of the British. A great shame it is to cloud their illusions of reality by referring them to the Grail legends indicating that Arthur was a "dweller at the Antipodes," i.e., at the tip of the *stauros*, *axis mundi*, or rotational pole of Planet Earth. Perry 200-01; Mustard and Passage xxxii. Add to that bit of trivia, Wolfram von Eschenbach's etymology for *Parzival*, in English "Perceval," which is *perce a val*, that is, "pierce through the middle" (Perry 201; Mustard & Passage xxxv, 78), and Goodrich's references to texts indicating that Perceval, like his father, Gawain, was "gigantic and bright or red-haired" (Goodrich 294) and we begin to see what Joseph Campbell knew but was unable to impart to Christian fundamentalists, who have no eyes to see or ears to hear.

175. Perry 206, 225-26, 239; Mustard & Passage 415; Bryant *Perlesvaus* 27, 80-81. Grail knights attending Grail processions invariably fail to ask what has come to be known as "the questions unasked." Grail-tale knights, like all good Christians, have been dissuaded from asking questions, and convinced simply to obey the commands of their civil and religious superiors. Moreover, Grail-tale knights are so hypnotized or narcotized by the grandeur of the Grail processions that their mindless stupor, in addition to their standing orders not to ask questions, paralyzes their rational intellects and mutes their mouths. Because they fail to ask the questions, they get unceremoniously and magically ejected from the Grail castle, and awake lying in the woods, much as drunken sailors who get thrown out of pubs sometimes awake in the gutter. Consumers of Grail literature are assured by Grail-tale authors that if only the knight had asked the "questions unasked," then all combats between Christian knights, and between Christian and Islamic knights, would have ceased, and the world would have flowered and the songbirds would have sung.

The allegory of the "questions unasked" is understandable to anyone who has progressed this far into this paper. Equate the Grail procession with the Mass. The solemn ceremonies of the Roman Catholic church and the established churches here in the British Isles are some of the best drama ever performed. A person need not have been raised in those churches to be speechless at the end of the Mass, Eucharist, or Communion Service. The pageantry and drama of the Mass fill up our senses and shift our reasoning powers into neutral, much as we become bereft of reason, yet supercharged with emotion, when we are in the presence of a person with whom we anticipate the pleasures of sexual intercourse. However, after we have seen **Figure 23** of this paper, our minds may be less ossified by dogma or paralyzed by emotions, and we may be able to understand that if the Grail knights had asked the questions, they might have found something else to fight about, but it is extremely unlikely that they would have continued fighting about line-form optical illusions that may be seen on the *greille*! They might, instead, have realized that Christianity is a new, improved, vegetation cult, and they might have become what we, today, would call "environmentalists."

176. Perry 267; Gantz *Mabinogion* 297.

177. What cauldron? **Figure 24.** And where is Bran's severed head? **Figure 25.** Nonsense? If so, it is not *my* nonsense! What it is, in my opinion, is an allegorical or metaphorical reference to a beautiful reality, i.e., the paradise that Planet Earth could become where humankind not filled with greed and hate.

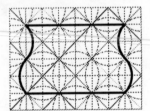

Figure 24

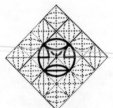

Figure 25

The Christian Church stopped teaching the Christ Story as cosmic allegory after the Church became the official religion of the Roman state, becoming syncretized (amalgamated) with the Sol Invictus cult and Mithraism, authoritarian cults which had molded the mindset of the common folk for military service in the Roman legions. The Roman state's hierarchy of St. Paul's Greco-Roman "Christianity" (Acts 11:26) soon abandoned the teachings of Jesus the Nazorean (John 19:19—correctly translated), who had promised to set people free. John 8:32. The message of the Nazorean *nabi* Yeshua ben Josef had been that each individual should find within himself the light of creation, and should seek cosmic oneness with the Creator and His creation. Gospel of Thomas 3,24,50,113. However, the Roman state wanted mindless foot soldiers—not contemplative peaceniks.

The Church Militant rewrote the Canonical Gospels, and issued marching orders to its Christian soldiers. (It could not rewrite the Gospel of Thomas, which was safely buried at Nag Hammadi until the middle of the twentieth century!) Introspection and logical analysis no longer were the *sine qua non* of the Christian true believer. Individualism was replaced with military-style group-think. The common folk were hammered incessantly with the message that unquestioning obedience to codes of belief and conduct was the only way toward salvation. Christian soldiers of Rome's legions were not annihilating the enemies of the power structure of the Roman state, in order to steal their lands and chattels. Rather, they were carrying the good news about Jesus Christ to the heathens—or so they were told. And so it remained when Spanish, French, and English Christians destroyed Native American cultures and millions of Native Americans in North, Central, and South America—not to steal gold and land but to save the souls of my great-grandmother's people. And so it is, today, in Bosnia-Hercegovina. And so it will remain, unless Christians stop parking their brains at the church door.

But the wonderful thing about truth is that it cannot be suppressed forever. Like a single blade of grass that lies dormant in a seed for many years, then bursts through a thick concrete slab, truth finds the light. Those of my readers who would prefer not to abandon Christianity have an opportunity to return to the quest of the pre-Roman Christians to find themselves, and to fit their lives into cosmic harmony with the Creator and His/Her Creation. The only requirement is that they must recall a modicum of their secondary-school algebra and geometry, or be willing to invest the time to recapture or to learn those mathematical skills. No amount of language skills, philosophy, or theology can open to moderns the doorway into what Bible authors meant by the *Logos* (John 1:1-5, 1:14) or the Mediator. 1 Timothy 2:5; Hebrews 9:15, 12:24. Only math skills will suffice because, as St. Augustine wrote, "[I]gnorance of number prevents us from understanding things that are set down in the scripture in a figurative and mystical way." Perry 198, 318; James 85.

If your Christian drill instructor insists that biblical numerology is nonsense, or is incomprehensible, ask him how he can say in one breath that the Bible is the historical, inerrant word of God, then say in the next breath that biblical numerology is nonsense! Ask him why biblical words can be understood, but biblical numerals cannot be. Then tell him you already know that biblical narratives are allegories which express the same mathematics used to erect the Gothic cathedrals. If he is seminary educated, you may be amazed at what he says when he knows you know what he knows.

Perry 286-347 discusses original Christianity as an extension of ancient mathematical crystallography and light physics, as do articles by David Fideler and Daniel Gautier in the Spring, 1993, edition of *Gnosis* magazine, No. 27, at pages 21-35. I will buy and read David Fideler's new book *Jesus Christ, Sun of God: Ancient Cosmology and Early Christian Symbolism*, when it is published by Quest Books in September, 1993. I recommend that my Christian readers who are tired of marching mindlessly to the drums of the Roman Church and its progeny, and who have eyes to see and ears to hear, should buy and read my book and his.

When an American newsman recently asked the Dalai Lama whether Christians should convert to Buddhism, he was dumfounded by the answer that each person should walk his own path to the summit of the mountain. You understand. Stay with Christianity or leave it. Truth is not in particular buildings. It is in you. Find it.

You have completed this short course, and it is time for your final examination. The drawing below is from the Book of Kells, circa 800 C.E., which resides at Trinity College, Dublin, in Ireland. Can you see the *greille*? The interference pattern? The concave-sided tetragon? Balder's mistletoe? Can you see Lion, Ox, Man, and Eagle? Man and ox are difficult, unless you look for the horned god, Cernunnos, the Celtic master of the animals of the circling cosmos, who became the model for the Christian devil when Jesus Christ took his job. Can you see the other face of the Celtic two-faced god? Can you see the other face of Christianity? There is even more to see, but you first must make yourself ready and able.

The Concilium of San Pietro
by
Charles Longstreet Weltner

with Foreword by
Lee Perry

Foreword

My mentor and friend, Charles Longstreet Weltner, the late Chief Justice of the Supreme Court of Georgia, tried to help me to publicize my book, *The Holy Grail, Cosmos of the Bible*, by giving copies of it to academicians and news reporters, and by explaining my speculations and evidence to them. In my words, not his, each professional religionist and news media representative to whom Charles tendered a copy of my book reacted like a Georgia mud turtle that suddenly had been awakened while sunning itself on a log in its favorite pond, i.e., each hissed, snapped his or her jaws threateningly, then dove for safety into the deep pools of religious consensus here in the Bible Belt of the Southern United States.

Continuing in my words, not his, the only safe way to feed an awakened Georgia mud turtle is to place the morsel on the end of a long stick, then to extend the tidbit right in front of the turtle's jaws. Either the turtle will snap it up, or will draw its head, feet, and tail within its hard shell and refuse to move an inch in any direction. Whenever I hear someone speak about hard-shelled religious fundamentalists, I think of my childhood experiences with Georgia mud turtles, as well as my experiences with the scowling and snapping old folks who attended the church of elderly frowns. My God laughs often.

I try to smile my way through life, no matter how badly my arthritis hurts.

But the academicians and reporters refused to bite. They remained within the protective shells of their religious beliefs.

So Charles cut himself a branch from the green wood of the tree of wisdom, with which to tickle the academic turtles' tails in order to tease them out of their shells. Once more, in my words, not his, the way you get a truculent turtle to taste the tidbit is to tickle its tail with one stick while you tender the tidbit with the other stick. The tail-tickled turtle pokes its head out of its shell, sees the tidbit as the enemy, snaps it from the stick, then decides, after all, that you are not the devil incarnate but a tenderer of tasty tidbits. It's a complex process, but it is worth the effort just to see the mud turtle smile. No kidding. Mud turtles, and fundamentalists, smile.

Not often. But they can.

The "Concilium of San Pietro" was Charles' tickling stick. My book was the tidbit.

But the academicians still refused to bite. They kept their heads in their shells, while hissing about the tickling Charles was giving them with the Concilium. You see, Charles knew the minds and methods of the professional religionists, having earned for himself a master's degree from a religious seminary, as well as two other earned master's degrees in law and Bible-era languages. Charles was working on his doctorate in Bible-era languages at Trinity College Dublin when cancer struck. He was what he wanted to be—a student to the very end. Tobacco killed my father, Ed, and my friend, Charles.

The Concilium, like the Grail tales, is a fiction based on a fact. The Concilium is a satire and parody about fictional theologians and exegetes who treat a discarded church raffle ticket actually found by Charles' daughter, June, on the sidewalk in front of the Central Presbyterian Church of Atlanta, Georgia, as a holy document that becomes venerated by the common folk because the academicians have spun around it a mystical web of scholarly nonsense—just like the Church has spun a web of scholarly nonsense around the *greille*, a plan and profile used by ancient builders to erect domes and vaults of rock, and used by ancient astronomers and navigators to find points in time-space on the known curvature of Planet Earth and on the posited firmament of Heaven. If endless scholarly debate and bottomless religious faith actually may spring forth from an ancient engineering drawing, then may not fictional faith be bottomed upon, and fictional debate swirl around, a discarded raffle ticket? The Holy Raffle Ticket instead of the Holy Grail? Charles, you were naughty, as well as brilliant!

When you, my reader, really understand the Concilium, you either will laugh or cry. The efforts of theologians and exegetes to know and to understand our Creator would be highly amusing had the consequences not been so devastating for humankind and the rest of God's creation.

Charles repeatedly tried to get the Concilium published in a wide variety of periodicals. Some editors declined publication because they did not understand it; others, because they did! The last time I saw Charles just a few hours before his death, I promised him that I would get the Concilium published. Here's one for you, my friend!

Charles wrote:

This is a report on the recent great Conference in Rome, which concluded on 3 IX 2187. But before addressing its apparent accomplishments, it may be that a brief review of the discovery and emergence of The Text (that being the subject matter of the Concilium) may be helpful.

Most people know that The Text was re-discovered two hundred years ago. It came to light almost casually, as did other great documentary discoveries of recent centuries. (In the 1890's, a peasant woman was digging by the Nile at Tell el-Amarna when her pick unearthed the first tablets of the diplomatic library of Pharaoh Ikhnaton. Two centuries ago, a Bedouin tossed a rock into the mouth of a cave in the Judean wilderness. The resulting sound of breaking pottery led him to the ancient library at Qumran, known as the "Dead Sea Scrolls." In the XXIst century, an ancient suburb of Damascus yielded up three Aramaic Gospels and the Hebrew text of the Book of Jubilees).

The re-discovery of The Text was not much different. A young girl, whose name is recorded only as "June," picked it up in the front of what was then a Protestant church in Atlanta, which is a town in the Southern United States. She showed it to her father. From that event, The Text—but three words long– came into the forefront of scholarly inquiry, veneration, and inevitable controversy.

The document itself is quite small—as are many of the ostraca found at archaeological sites in the Ancient Near East. It measures but 52 mm X 26 mm, and is now lodged permanently within the Vatican.

German theologians were the first to proclaim The Text as a unity, encompassing a tri-partite theology, which they have designated as *Scherz, Dienst und Erlösung* (Joy, Servanthood, and Salvation—this last term sometimes being translated as "Redemption," which is the literal English of The Text).

These early interpreters soon came under fire from another group who, calling themselves Binominalists (as opposed to the "Trinominalist" first commentators), insisted that the first term of The Text is not a noun, but a modifier of the second term– hence the text has but two, and not three, nouns. *Scherz* (joy), they insisted, must be understood as *freudig* (joyful), so that the first of only *two* nouns is to be understood as "joyful servitude." The Binominalists declared the text to be of a genre with the Servant Songs of Deutero-Isaiah.

A Swedish group at Uppsala, later becoming known as the "N-V-O" (for noun-verb-object) insisted that The Text has but one noun, which is third in a chain, following the initial subject and the medial verb. The true meaning must be this: it is *Joy* that facilitates (the original English word is "Services") Redemption. A related element of the N-V-O in Austria has published a learned journal, which is styled simply *die Freude* (the joy), after their understanding of the first term.

Several American textual scholars have examined the text and suggest an emendation to the first term (which is the rather non-scientific word, "Fun") by adding a final *d*, which they insist has dropped out through scribal error. They would interpret the first term, thus emended, as an imperative. It is their contention that the sense of The Text, and its *Gattung*, must lead inevitably to understanding it as a *command* to followers, stressing the primacy of offerings for the maintenance of the *cultus*. Their principal support for this interpretation is the widespread and heavily-documented "televangelicalism" of the XXth century. (There was, of course, incessant usage of the verb "to fund," having the sense of supplying financial support.)

A small group of Hebrew scholars centered at the ancient site of Jamnia (sometimes called Jabne, Javneh) points to a little-noted series of digits, appended to The Text, as follows: "0220707." They suggest that this could be a Kabbalah-like symbol for *Shalom*, in the sense of "completion." The 022, they say, is the number of the letters in the Hebrew alphabet. This is followed by the appearance of the string "0707," which is understood as the "perfect number," seven. Then, they maintain, for even greater an emphasis, the entire numerical *catena* is doubled. (That is, it appears *bis* on the face of The Text, placed vertically in both margins.)

A Russian historian, in a radical rejection of all religious signification of The Text, has suggested that the three words are only proper names, and that the Text is in actuality a personal identification card. He points to the earlier popularity as proper names of Prudence, Constance, and Joy (the very first term of the Text). This hypothesis has drawn little support, however, as the so-called "Social Security" numbers of the United States during that era had at least 9 digits. (This factor, however, would not exclude the idea of a personal identification card reflecting membership in a group sufficiently small to be served by 7 digit identification numbers.) Additionally, he generally is thought to rely too heavily upon the term "Joy" as a proper name, because "Joy" in reality is not the English word, but a retrojection of the German translation through the term "*Scherz*." The Text, of course, is in English, and we have no documentation of the first term ("Fun") as an *Eigenname* of the period.

That, however, is background, most of which is quite familiar. The divergences outlined above impelled Pope Iskandr Mbolo Nguyen IV to convene the Concilium in the Basilica of San Pietro. The Call cited the urgency of achieving a greater degree of hermeneutical commonality as regards The Text. Among the twenty-three hundred conferees were substantial delegations of Trinominalists, Binominalists, N-V-O's and Shalomites. But the desired unity proved elusive. When the Concilium was nearing its conclusion, a new schism developed among a small element that had come together under the banner of *Officia* (thus stressing the importance of the second term of The Text, "Services"). These, in turn, fell into discord in a disputation relative to the *kind* of "Services" contemplated in The Text, i.e., whether liturgical forms or eleemosynary structures.

The Concilium ended on what seemed to be a note of forced harmony and false ecumenism. The Pontiff's valedictory found cause for optimism only in observing that the delegates had traveled from the far corners of the Earth; had reasoned together; and would return to their homelands "strengthened by the realization that the search for Truth knows no national boundaries, and that it will endure."

It is not unrealistic to suggest that dissension and discord, as well, will endure. The Text remains, of course, central to most of the inheritors of the Judaeo-Christian traditions. But it remains also as the subject of wildly variant interpretations.

Yet, it is a sign of maturity in human intercourse that so differing a set of beliefs can emerge surrounding a single brief source (even as Jews, Christians, and Muslims claim their origins from the same Father Abraham), and that these divergences have produced no *jihad* thus far into the Twenty-second Century. Considering the religious wars that have plagued Mankind forever, that is solid cause for hope!

This report will conclude in the usual manner—with the words that have led us, for two hundred years, into new albeit diverse avenues of self-understanding. It ends with the words of The Text itself, which is a guide for all of Humankind, as we approach the Twenty-third Century: Fun Services Redemption.

Respectfully,

Chaim Eudo Robson
Delegate at Large, USA
Trinominal Synod South
Dated: 17 IX 2187

Post Scriptum

There is a curious reference in the addenda to the Official Report of Proceedings of the Concilium of San Pietro. It relates to a person, without credentials, but listed as Observer, who attended all sessions, and generally was considered by the delegates as mildly deranged. He was a citizen of Milano, and introduced himself only as "Tonio."[1] Hence, the Official Report lists him without further elucidation as "Tonio il Milaneso." Your reporter saw him frequently. He carried with him at all times (and displayed to whomever he might) a "Scrapbook," which evidently was a large, blank portfolio, popular in Twentieth-century America as a means of preserving memorabilia. This document, he said, came to him several decades ago from an aged and distant cousin in Atlanta, USA (coincidentally, the *locus* of The Text's recovery) who had received it from his great-great-great-grandfather. Among other items, many of which are incomprehensible, is a small printed tractate containing The Text. Beneath it is written in a crude hand: "First ticket sold (by me to me) as Annual Jaycees Circus chairman, summer of 1957. Doorprize—transistor radio—won by Gober Huckeba."

Quite naturally, no one paid Tonio any heed. The terms of the handwriting made no sense. (What, for example, is an "Annual Jaycees?" Or, what is a "Gober Huckeba?" The words are those of The Text, it is true (i.e., "Fun Services Redemption"), but the digits ("0261414") are radically different, and from a numerological standpoint are meaningless. Tonio's incessant prattle stretched credulity, and all who were burdened with Tonio rejected his arguments. So *il Milaneso* was dismissed as a sincere but misguided soul, whose remote American ancestor likely treasured and safeguarded a copy of The Text during his youth. That is nothing unusual. Almost every *m'zuzah* of the present time contains The Text.

---

1. By Lee Perry: Any resemblance between the fictional "Tonio" and me is *not* coincidental!

Bibliography

Allen, Richard Hinckley. *Star Names: Their Lore And Meaning*. Dover Publications, Inc., New York, 1963.

Angus, S. *The Mystery-Religions: A Study In The Religious Background Of Early Christianity*. Dover Publications, Inc., New York, 1975.

Aristeas, The Letter Of. See *Forgotten Books of Eden, The*.

Arnheim, Michael. *Is Christianity True?* Duckworth, London, 1984.

Aveni, Anthony F. *Skywatchers Of Ancient Mexico*. University of Texas Press, Austin, 1980.

Baigent, Michael; Richard Leigh; and Henry Lincoln. *Holy Blood, Holy Grail*. Dell Publishing Co., Inc., New York, 1983.

Baigent, Michael; and Richard Leigh. *The Dead Sea Scrolls Deception*. Jonathan Cape, London, 1991.

Baigent, Michael; Richard Leigh; and Henry Lincoln. *The Messianic Legacy*. Jonathan Cape, London, 1986.

Baigent, Michael; and Richard Leigh. *The Temple and the Lodge*. Arcade Publishing, New York, 1989.

Beckmann, Petr. *A History of Pi*. Dorset Press, New York, 1971.

Bible, King James Version.

Bible, The New English, With The Apocrypha, Oxford Study Edition. Oxford University Press, Inc., New York, 1976.

Branston, Brian. *The Lost Gods Of England*. Oxford University Press, New York, 1974.

Brennan, Martin. *The Stars And The Stones*. Thames and Hudson, New York, 1983.

Brooke, Rosalind and Christopher. *Popular Religion In The Middle Ages: Western Europe 1000-1300.* Thames and Hudson Ltd., New York, 1984.

Brown, Peter Lancaster. *Megaliths and Masterminds.* Robert Hale Limited, London, 1979.

Bryant, Nigel.(Translator.) *The High Book Of The Grail: A Translation Of The Thirteenth Century Romance of Perlesvaus.* Rowman and Littlefield, Totowa, New Jersey, 1978.

Bryant, Nigel. (Translator.) See Chrétien de Troyes.

Budge, E.A. Wallis, Sir. *Osiris & The Egyptian Resurrection.* Dover Publications, Inc., New York, 1973.

Campbell, Joseph. *The Hero With A Thousand Faces.* Princeton University Press, Princeton, 1973.

Cavendish, Richard. *An Illustrated Encyclopedia Of Mythology.* Orbis Publishing Limited, London, 1980.

Chrétien de Troyes. *Perceval: The Story of the Grail.* Translated by Bryant, Nigel. D.S. Brewer, Cambridge, 1982.

Chrétien de Troyes. *Yvain, Or The Knight With The Lion.* Translated by Cline, Ruth Harwood. The University of Georgia Press, Athens, Georgia, 1984.

Cirlot, J.E. *A Dictionary Of Symbols.* Second Edition. Philosophical Library, Inc., New York, 1983.

Cline, Ruth Harwood. (Translator.) See Chrétien de Troyes.

Cohen, Edmund D. *The Mind of the Bible-Believer.* Prometheus Books, Buffalo, New York, 1988.

Cross, Tom Peete, and Clark Harris Slover. *Ancient Irish Tales.* Henry Holt and Company, Inc., New York, 1936.

Crossley-Holland, Kevin. (Translator.) *The Norse Myths.* Andre Deutsch Limited, London, 1980.

Cumont, Franz. *The Mysteries Of Mithra*. Dover Publications, Inc., New York, 1956.

Cumont, Franz. *The Oriental Religions In Roman Paganism*. Dover Publications, New York, 1956.

Currer-Briggs, Noel. *The Shroud and the Grail*. George Weidenfeld & Nicolson, London, 1987.

Davidson, H.R. Ellis. *Gods And Myths Of The Viking Age*. Bell Publishing Company, New York, 1981.

De Bhaldraithe, Tomás. *English-Irish Dictionary*. Oifig An tSoláthair, Baile Átha Cliath, Éire, 1959.

Dinneen, Rev. Patrick S. *Foclóir Gaedhilge Agus Béarla* (Irish-English Dictionary). The Irish Texts Society, Dublin, 1927.

Dobin, Joel C., Rabbi.*The Astrological Secrets Of The Hebrew Sages: To Rule Both Day And Night*. Inner Traditions International, Ltd., New York, 1983.

Dreyer, J.L.E. *A History Of Astronomy From Thales To Kepler*. Dover Publications, Inc., New York, 1953.

Eisenman, Robert; and Michael Wise. *The Dead Sea Scrolls Uncovered*. Element, Longmead, Shaftesbury, Dorset, UK, 1992.

Eschenbach, Wolfram von. *Parzival*. Translated by Mustard, Helen M., and Charles E. Passage. Alfred A. Knopf, Inc., and Random House, Inc., New York, 1961.

Eschenbach, Wolfram von. *Willehalm*. Translated by Gibbs, Marion E., and Sidney M. Johnson. Penguin Books, Harmondsworth, Middlesex, UK, 1984.

Eusebius. *The History Of The Church*. Translated by Williamson, G.A. Penguin Books Ltd., Harmondsworth, Middlesex, UK, 1983.

Evans, H. Meurig. (Editor.) *Y Geiriadur Cymraeg Cyfoes* (The Dictionary of Modern Welsh), Hughes a'i Fab (Cyhoeddwyr) Cyf., Llandybie, Cymru, 1981.

Evans, Sebastian. (Translator.) *The High History Of The Holy Grail*. The Attic Press, Inc., Greenwood, South Carolina, 1969.

Fanning, A.E. *Planets, Stars And Galaxies: Descriptive Astronomy For Beginners*. Dover Publications, Inc., New York, 1966.

Farbridge, Maurice H. (Edited by Harry M. Orlinsky.) *Studies In Biblical And Semitic Symbolism*. KTAV Publishing House, Inc., New York, 1970.

Forgotten Books Of Eden, The. Bell Publishing Company, New York, 1981.

Fox, Matthew. (Translator.) *Breakthrough: Meister Eckhart's Creation Spirituality in New Translation*. Doubleday, New York, 1980.

Fox, Matthew. (Editor.) (Herein referenced "1 Fox.") *Illuminations of Hildegard of Bingen*. Bear & Company, Inc., Santa Fe, 1985.

Fox, Matthew. (Editor.) (Herein referenced "2 Fox.") *Hildegard of Bingen's Book of Divine Works*. Bear & Company, Inc., Santa Fe, 1987.

Frankfort, Henri; H.A. Frankfort; John A. Wilson; Thorkild Jacobsen; and William A. Irwin. *The Intellectual Adventure Of Ancient Man*. The University of Chicago Press, Chicago, 1977.

Frazer, James G. *The Golden Bough: The Roots Of Religion And Folklore*. Avenel Books, New York, 1981.

Gantz, Jeffrey. (Translator.) *Early Irish Myths And Sagas*. Dorset Press, New York, 1985.

Gantz, Jeffrey. (Translator.) *The Mabinogion*. Dorset Press, New York, 1985.

Gibbs, Marion E.; and Sidney M. Johnson. (Translators.) See Eschenbach, Wolfram von.

Ghyka, Matila. *The Geometry Of Art And Life*. Dover Publications, Inc., New York, 1977.

Gillings, Richard J. *Mathematics In The Time Of The Pharaohs*. Dover Publications, Inc., New York, 1982.

Gimpel, Jean. *The Cathedral Builders*. Grove Press, Inc., New York, 1983.

Godwin, Joscelyn. *Mystery Religions In The Ancient World*. Harper & Row, Publishers, Inc., San Francisco, 1981.

Goodrich, Norma Lorre. *The Holy Grail*. HarperCollins Publishers, New York, 1992.

Graham, Lloyd M. *Deceptions And Myths Of The Bible*. Bell Publishing Company, New York, 1979.

Graves, Robert, and Raphael Patai. *Hebrew Myths: The Book Of Genesis*. Greenwich House, New York, 1983.

Greeley, Andrew M. *Myths of Religion*. Warner Books, New York, 1989.

Guest, Charlotte, Lady. (Translator.) *The Mabinogion*. John Jones Cardiff Ltd., Cardiff, Wales, 1977.

Hadingham, Evan. *Early Man And The Cosmos*. William Heinemann Ltd., London, 1983.

Hamilton, Bernard. *The Medieval Inquisition*. Holmes & Meier Publishers, Inc., New York, 1981.

Hapgood, Charles H. *Maps Of The Ancient Sea Kings: Evidence Of Advanced Civilization In The Ice Age*. E. P. Dutton, New York, 1979.

Hawkins, Gerald S., and John B. White. *Stonehenge Decoded*. Doubleday & Company, Inc., Garden City, 1965.

Heafford, Philip. *Fun With Mathematics*. Bell Publishing Company, New York, 1983.

Heath, Thomas, Sir. *A History Of Greek Mathematics*. Dover Publications, Inc., New York, 1981.

Heath, Thomas, Sir. *Aristarchus Of Samos*. Dover Publications, Inc., New York, 1981.

Hermas, Book Of The Shepherd Of. See *Lost Books Of The Bible, The*.

Hollander, Lee M. (Translator). *The Poetic Edda*, Second Edition, Revised. University of Texas Press, Austin, 1987.

Howarth, Stephen. *The Knights Templar*. Dorset Press, New York, 1991.

Hoyle, Fred, Sir. *On Stonehenge*. W. H. Freeman and Company, San Francisco, 1977.

Hozeski, Bruce. *Hildegard of Bingen's Scivias*. Bear & Company, Inc., Santa Fe, 1986.

James, John. *Chartres: The Masons Who Built A Legend*. Routledge & Kegan Paul, London, 1985.

Jones-Wake. See *Lost Books of the Bible, The*.

Jung, C.J. *Mandala Symbolism*. Princeton University Press, Princeton, 1973.

Kramer, Samuel Noah. *The Sumerians: Their History, Culture, and Character*. The University of Chicago Press, Chicago, 1963.

Krupp, E.C. *Echoes Of The Ancient Skies: The Astronomy Of Lost Civilizations*. Harper & Row, Publishers, New York, 1983.

Langdon, S. *The Babylonian Epic Of Creation*. Clarendon Press, Oxford, 1923.

Langdon, Stephen Herbert. Volume V, Semitic. *The Mythology Of All Races*. Cooper Square Publishers, New York, 1964.

Lawlor, Robert. *Sacred Geometry*. The Crossroad Publishing Company, New York, 1982.

Lawrence, J. Dennis. *A Catalog of Special Plane Curves*. Dover Publications, Inc., New York, 1972.

Lorayne, Harry, and Jerry Lucas. *The Memory Book.* Ballantine Books, New York, 1986.

Lost Books Of The Bible, The. Bell Publishing Company, New York, 1979.

Lubicz. See Schwaller de Lubicz, R.A.

Malone, Dumas; Robert Llewellyn; and Charles Granquist. *Thomas Jefferson's Monticello.* Thomasson-Grant, Inc., Charlottesville, Virginia, 1983.

Matthews, John. (Editor.) *An Arthurian Reader.* The Aquarian Press, Wellingborough, Northamptonshire, UK, 1988.

Mccoby, Hyam. *The Mythmaker: Paul and the Invention of Christianity,* Harper & Row, Publishers, San Francisco, 1986.

McMann, Jean. *Riddles Of The Stone Age: Rock Carvings Of Ancient Europe.* Thames and Hudson Ltd., London, 1980.

Meyer, Marvin W. (Editor) *The Ancient Mysteries: A Sourcebook.* Harper & Row, Publishers, New York, 1987.

Minnaert, M. *The Nature Of Light & Color In The Open Air.* Dover Publications, Inc., New York, 1954.

Morison, Samuel Eliot. *The European Discovery Of America: The Northern Voyages A.D. 500-1600.* Oxford University Press, New York, 1971.

Mustard, Helen M.; and Charles E. Passage. (Translators.) See Eschenbach, Wolfram von.

Neugebauer, O. *The Exact Sciences In Antiquity.* Second Edition. Dover Publications, Inc., New York, 1969.

Oates, Joan. *Babylon.* Thames and Hudson Ltd., London, 1979.

Oldenbourg, Zoé. *Massacre At Montségur.* Dorset Press, New York, 1990.

Oxford English Dictionary, The Compact Edition of the. Oxford University Press, New York, 1971.

Partner, Peter. *The Murdered Magicians*. The Aquarian Press, Rochester, Vermont, 1987.

Perry, Lee. *The Holy Grail, Cosmos of the Bible*. Philosophical Library, New York, 1991.

Perry, Lee. *Hildegard von Bingen: Hierophant of the Holy Grail*. LazerAge, Atlanta, 1992. [A paper presented to the International Society of Hildegard von Bingen Studies during the 27th International Congress on Medieval Studies, May 7-10, 1992, at Kalamazoo, Michigan, U.S.A.]

Perry, Lee. *Brains Unchained: Finding the Holy Grail and Christianity's Visionary Origins*. LazerAge, Atlanta, 1992. [A paper presented to the 1992 International Forum on New Science, September 16-20, 1992, Fort Collins, Colorado, U.S.A.]

Platt & Brett. See *Forgotten Books Of Eden, The*.

Rey, H.A. *The Stars: A New Way To See Them*. Houghton Mifflin Company, Boston, 1976.

Robbins, Rossell Hope. *The Encyclopedia Of Witchcraft & Demonology*. Bonanza Books, New York, 1981.

Ronan, Colin. *Lost Discoveries*. Bonanza Books, New York, 1981.

Saggs, H.W.F. *The Greatness That Was Babylon*. Hawthorn Books, Inc., Publishers, New York, 1962.

Schwaller de Lubicz. R.A. *The Temple In Man: Sacred Architecture And The Perfect Man*. Inner Traditions International, New York, 1977.

Service, Alastair, and Jean Bradbery.*Megaliths and Their Mysteries*. Macmillan Publishing Co., Inc., New York, 1979.

Sheehan, Thomas. *The First Coming: How the Kingdom of God Became Christianity*. Random House, New York, 1986.

Sinclair, Andrew. *The Sword and the Grail*. Crown Publishers, New York, 1992.

Smith, Morton. *Jesus The Magician*. Harper & Row, Publishers, San Francisco, 1981.

Spong, John Shelby, The Right Reverend. *Rescuing the Bible from Fundamentalism: A Bishop Rethinks the Meaning of Scripture*. HarperSanFrancisco, 1991.

Talbott, David N. *The Saturn Myth*. Doubleday & Company, Inc., Garden City, 1980.

Tedlock, Dennis. (Translator.) *Popol Vuh*. Simon & Schuster, Inc., New York, 1985.

Tribbe, Frank C. *Portrait Of Jesus? The Illustrated Story Of The Shroud Of Turin*. Stein and Day, Publishers, New York, 1983.

Walker, Benjamin. *Gnosticism*. The Aquarian Press, Wellingborough, Northamptonshire, UK, 1983.

Washburn, Mark. *In The Light Of The Sun: From Sunspots To Solar Energy*. Harcourt Brace Jovanovich, New York, 1981.

Webster's Third New International Dictionary Unabridged, G. & C. Merriam Company, Springfield, Massachusetts, 1966.

Willehalm. See Chrétien de Troyes.

Williamson, G.A. See Eusebius.

Wilson, Ian. *Jesus: The Evidence*. Harper & Row, San Francisco, 1984.

Wood, Elizabeth A. *Crystals And Light: An Introduction To Optical Crystallography*. Second Revised Edition. Dover Publications, Inc., New York, 1977.

Wood, John Edwin. *Sun, Moon And Standing Stones*. Oxford University Press, Oxford, 1980.

Yarwood, Doreen. *The Architecture Of Europe*. Chancellor Press, London, 1974.

Periodicals

Deacon, A. Bernard. "Geometrical Drawings From Malekula And Other Islands Of The New Hebrides." *The Journal of the Royal Anthropological Institute*, 1934, Vol. 64, pages 129-176.

Nissen, Phillip. "Sand Drawings of Vanuatu." *Mathematics in a Multicultural Society*, 1988, pages 34-39, The Mathematical Association, Leicester, UK.

Roberts, David. "In France, an ordeal by fire and a monster weapon called 'Bad Neighbor'", *Smithsonian*, Vol. 22, No. 2.

Rowe, Veronica. "The Weave of Wonderment," *Ireland of the Welcomes*, Vol. 41, No. 6, November-December, 1992.

Weltner, Charles Longstreet. "The Heavens Of Babylon—Ezekiel's Vision And The Trisection Problem." *Congressional Record*, Vol. 125, No. 89, June 29, 1979, pages E3384-E3387.